The Congregation Driven Ministry

The Congregation Driven Ministry

Moving from Membership to Maturity

Dr. Larry W. Ellis

iUniverse, Inc.
New York Lincoln Shanghai

The Congregation Driven Ministry
Moving from Membership to Maturity

iUniverse books may be ordered through booksellers or by contacting:

iUniverse
2021 Pine Lake Road, Suite 100
Lincoln, NE 68512
www.iuniverse.com
1-800-Authors (1-800-288-4677)

Because of the dynamic nature of the Internet, any Web addresses or links contained in this book may have changed since publication and may no longer be valid.

The views expressed in this work are solely those of the author and do not necessarily reflect the views of the publisher, and the publisher hereby disclaims any responsibility for them.

ISBN: 978-0-595-43523-4 (pbk)
ISBN: 978-0-595-87849-9 (ebk)

Printed in the United States of America

Dedicated to the fond memory of

Deacon John A. Prothro, Sr.

A servant of God and a friend to the pastor

Contents

Acknowledgements

The completion of this volume spans work done for more than a decade. It began as an effort to challenge myself to believe that congregations could grow without compromise. The gospel is enough. Thurman White and Sherman Anderson co-taught these principles with me in several Bay Area churches with ample success. I am indebted to them beyond measure. Further, the men and women of Pilgrim Baptist Church have permitted me to "test" this work on them without complaint. I bless the Lord for them, for they are a great people! Tynetta Brooks and Joann Griffin have rendered more support than I could have expected. The Reverend Henry L. Perkins was kind enough to allow me to share this concept with The First Baptist Church of Pittsburg, California on several occasions. I cannot thank him and them enough. I want to thank Paulette Sylvester of A Total Office Service for her editing skill, word processing and belief in this project upon reading it. Finally, my wife, Van and my adult children, Tawana, Justin and Austin are my earthly pride and joy. May this work find its way into the hearts and ministries of many ... to the glory of God.

Foreword

It has been amazing watching the manifestation of God's gift unfold through the life of a servant such as Dr. Larry Wayne Ellis.

Dr. Ellis has been a blessing to the larger kingdom of Christianity as he unselfishly shares himself with others.

The concept of The Congregation Driven Ministry is one I recommend to every pastor and/or church leadership team. If you are interested in developing a ministry driven by purpose rather than personality, The Congregation Driven Ministry is the design to embrace.

First Baptist Church of Pittsburg, California now enjoys the fruit and labor of approximately six (6) years of intentional training to affect our community using this design. The Congregation Driven Ministry model equips leaders for purpose, passion, and productivity. Pastors and leaders become partners in ministry! Functionality among the saints is experienced as workers are driven to a more intimate relationship with God through faith in Christ Jesus!

It calls for a commitment of time, talent, and treasure as necessary components to facilitate this practical ministry model.

- The Congregation Driven Ministry establishes longevity, succession, and purpose for the life of church ministry.
- Equipping God's people to do ministry in the 21st Century, so the church, becomes "essential" as purpose and passion becomes the driving force.

In regards to equipping God's people, you will discover as you read The Congregation Driven Ministry the discipline, depth, and commitment which Dr. Ellis has given in developing such a paradigm.

In the larger context of Christian ministry, we salute Dr. Larry Wayne Ellis for his marvelous mind, mission, and vision toward the work of *"total inclusion"* in the body of Christ.

Making Disciples for Our Savior,
Rev. Henry L. Perkins

Preface

"The Congregation Driven Ministry"

I am thankful, honored and humbled to have the privilege of writing this Preface for my Pastor's book, *The Congregation Driven Ministry* (CDM). Thankful because by the grace of God, I am saved and was led to Pilgrim Baptist Church some 17 years ago to renew my walk with the Lord. There I met Pastor Ellis, who has since been my Pastor, friend and mentor. I am honored that Pastor Ellis thought enough of me, on behalf of our members, to ask me to write this Preface. Humbled because I know that the concepts embodied in *The Congregation Driven Ministry* (along with the prayerful study of God's Word) will help many hundreds, if not thousands, of Christians the world over to grow spiritually and help many churches to become more productive in their ministry efforts—all to the glory of God.

I have experienced firsthand how The Congregation Driven Ministry works. CDM has helped me to mature as both a lay Christian leader and a secular business CEO. For the Trustee Ministry in which I've led and been actively involved, CDM provided fresh insights to help us to truly recognize our role as servants (and not overseers). In the context of the church's mission, CDM clarified that our Trustees' primary function is to help fund the Pastor's vision for the church, and to fund and support various ministries to meet people's needs. I have also had the opportunity to lead CDM workshops at other churches. In these sessions, I've witnessed how CDM can energize struggling ministries and their members, offering an actionable vision for what God wants his church and each of its ministry leaders to become. The role definition, mission clarity and teamwork emphasis CDM offers is vital to the success of any organization—whether it be the church or a multi-billion dollar corporation. Why is The Congregation Driven Ministry concept so effective? Because it provides a sound biblically-based framework for ministry that clarifies certain fundamental concepts—for example, that every child of God who confesses Jesus Christ as Lord and Savior has value; that the church should meet the needs of all members; that every member should be considered to be a minister and, therefore, accountable to use his/her spiritual gifts to serve in ministry to help the Church to prepare the saints for ministry and to reach the unsaved.

Many times we confess Christ but then we become confused about what to do next? How do we continue to grow spiritually? Many pastors and their churches also seem to grow to a certain point then plateau and become spiritually stagnant, lacking a clear vision for how to take their ministries to the next level of development. *The Congregation Driven Ministry* provides a set of "best practices" for clergy and laity, so both are clear about their respective ministry roles and both can better understand how to grow spiritually, lead effectively and live more victoriously.

The Holy Spirit, God's Word and CDM work together to provide all you need to grow as a Christian, for your church to transform lives and to produce more ministerial fruit. I am thankful to God for giving Pastor Ellis this original vision. CDM can help you whether you're a lay or secular leader. As you read through this book and work with these concepts, I pray that you'll be as blessed as the many members of Pilgrim Baptist Church and other churches have been over the years that have embraced CDM.

May His grace and peace be yours in abundance,
Thurman V. White, Jr.
Member, Pilgrim Baptist Church, San Mateo, California

The Introduction

The Church of Jesus Christ is mired in mediocrity. I believe the reason for this prevailing mediocrity is that the Church has become committed to making celebrities and not disciples committed to Christ. In The Congregation Driven Ministry, the emphasis is on empowering the laity. It does not seek to minimize the authority of the pastor, but it seeks to return the Church to the biblical mandate to make disciples. I believe that the Church's current fascination with celebrities is because the Church has lost its identity. The Church is the Body of Christ. It belongs to the Lord Jesus Christ who is the head. But modern society has minimized the Person of Christ, so the Church is seeking to find an identity that is acceptable to the world to give it a sense of meaning or purpose. The result is that the Church is usually personality driven and not Christ centered. In its fulfillment, The Congregation Driven Ministry is a ministry of healing—bringing the Church to its place of wholeness. There are five areas of concern as it relates to the Church's leadership.

The first area is pride. Because of pride many pastors are consumed with making a name for themselves and not making a name for Christ. Pride seeks to find glory in one's self and not give the glory to God. When pastors seek to be celebrities, they then minimize the place of Christ and maximize their own place and the Bible clearly says that "pride goes before the fall."

Secondly, there is the area of praise. When pastors are gifted and some are gifted in many areas, it tends to focus the attention on the pastor and not on Christ. So the congregation seems to want to lift up the name of the leader rather than lift up the Name of Christ. The Church's energy then goes to promote the ministry of the leader, thus, making the Church personality-driven and not Christ-centered.

The third area of concern for leaders is popularity. Popularity seeks to make us people pleasers and not God pleasers. When one seeks to be popular, they will often minimize the difficult things in the gospel and begin to say what the congregation wants to hear. Paul said that in the last days the membership would have itching ears and they would gather to themselves teachers that will say what they want to hear. (2 Tim. 4:1-5)

Fourthly, there is the concern of personhood. Many ministers today are basing their ministry on the size of their compensation package. Money becomes the measure of ministry. This is not an indictment on those ministers who are growing, who are God-honoring and Christ-leading, but this is an indictment on those who base the worth of their ministry and their personal worth on the size of their compensation package or Church.

I believe that the concern of pride, personal praise, popularity and personhood leads to the fifth area of concern and that is promiscuity. It is a well-known fact that many of the leading ministers, not only in the Catholic Church but in the Evangelical Movement, are caught in promiscuity. The desire to be popular and the desire to have their names in light has led to an almost "groupie mentality" among ministers. This is an area of grave concern. Promiscuity is an indication that a ministry is involved in fleshly pursuits and not spiritual pursuits.

These are our concerns and The Congregation Driven Ministry seeks to address these concerns by focusing on the person of Christ and the work of ministry, not on the pastor.

The function of ministry is modeling. There are five things that must be modeled, if one is to be a minister of Christ.

The first function is the message. The bible is clear in that no human has the authority to change the message. The message that we are to preach is not our message, it is a message that was delivered to us by the Lord. "We preach Christ and him crucified." (1 Cor. 1:23) The message is important because the message is to be a saving message, a healing message, a delivering message, a life changing message. The only message that has the power to change lives is the message that Jesus Christ is Lord. The leader must model the message. They are not only to lip the message, they are to live the message. Paul states in Romans 1:16, "I am not ashamed of the Gospel of Jesus Christ. It is the power of God that is the salvation to the Jew and to the Greek." This message changed Paul. It changed the early Church. It has changed men and women throughout Christendom. But the message is only able to change when it is Christ centered. Jesus said, "If I be lifted up, I will draw all men unto me."

Thus, the primary function of leadership is modeling the message of Jesus Christ.

Secondly, the function of leadership is the mission. (Matthew 28:18-20). Often in today's Church it is a "come ye" philosophy and not a "go ye" philosophy. In other words, we are to stand on the promises and not just sit on the premises. The Church has become static and not dynamic. We are building ministries that are saying, "Come to the Church and see what we are doing," rather than the biblical message of, "Go out and make disciples of all nations". The message is mission-oriented. We are to take the Word to everyone. It is a "whosoever will" message.

The third function of leadership is motivation, First Corinthians 15:58. The motivation is that the ministry that we have is so important that we will not allow any one or any thing to distract us from this message. Paul says in First Corinthians 15 that "our labor in the Lord is not in vain." When we do ministry, whether it is a ministry that is characterized by numerical growth or qualitative growth, the motivation is not size but quality. We are motivated because we must all stand before the judgement seat of Christ and give an account of what we do in our ministry.

The fourth function of leadership is ministry, Second Corinthians 4:1-7. "Since we have this ministry, as we have received mercy we do not lose heart." We have this ministry as a great gift. All of us remember a time when Christ was not in our life. And since we are saved, we now are to be involved in a ministry that ultimately gives others a chance to hear the Good News of the Gospel of Jesus Christ.

The final function of leadership is maturity. According to James 1:6, it is not enough to receive Christ. The believer is to engage in the process of sanctification. The Lord desires that His Church be motivated to maturity. Paul says in the letter to the Ephesians that we are to no longer be tossed to and fro by every wind of doctrine but we are to come to that place in our lives where we are steadfast and unmovable, always abounding in the Lord's work. We are to become mature believers.

How do we actualize this ministry that seeks to make Jesus Christ Lord? What is it that we need to do? The first thing that we must admit is that any ministry that is based on change is going to be resisted. Change is resisted because we are comfortable with what is familiar to us. The Church is called to change. We are to engage in methodologies that can bring people in closer alignment with the Person of Christ. We do not change the message, but the context of the message must change to meet the needs of each generation. The Church is to be a change agent, Luke 5:1-11. We must admit that people resist change. Change is a threat. Change requires that we modify ourselves. Change means a loss of control. Change means letting God lead. Change means to grow. Change requires cooperation. Change requires teamwork. Change requires pastoral vision and congregational support. Change can be frightening.

The Congregation Driven Ministry again is, therefore, a fulfillment of a ministry of change and of healing. It is to bring a sense of wholeness to the congregation. We must address the biblical basis of this ministry. Here are some passages that we will discuss: Matthew 12:10-16; Mark 1:32-34; and Luke 4:37-44. In looking at these we are going to assess five things that the Church must have in order for this ministry to be effective.

Every Church and every ministry within the Church must have a mission statement. The mission statement, of course, is based on Matthew 28:18-20. But within that, each ministry must understand that their statement must fall under the auspices of Matthew 28.

As a mission statement, the membership is to be encouraged to use their spiritual gifts in ministry. Each member must understand that he or she is not saved to sit but saved to serve and it is their responsibility to discover their purpose and their gifts and then use those gifts in ministry.

We are commissioned by God to magnify God through Jesus Christ. This means that when members are in ministry, they will magnify or make larger the Kingdom of God. The member is to seek the Kingdom of God where they live, where they labor, where they learn and where they spend their leisure time. These are all areas that they are to show forth the reality of Kingdom living. The whole value of this ministry is to encourage each individual to mature in their own walk with God, ensuring that the ministry again is not personality driven but Spirit led.

What are the means for this to happen? It is by meeting the needs of each age group through a comprehensive program of preaching, teaching, workshops and conferences. The goal is to nurture existing relationships and create new ones that will assist in meeting the Church's objectives. In constructing an organization strategy and philosophy that will reflect our agreed upon goals and objectives, each member is invaluable and a necessary part of the ministry plan and must commit him or herself to the vision by using their gifts in ministry.

Let's look at some suggestions to make ministry happen. When you look at a congregation that is growing quantitatively and qualitatively, what is going on in that ministry? The Congregation Driven Ministry is a way to assess that. Here are some things that we know makes ministry happen.

We are to establish priorities. In every ministry, first things must be first. Every ministry has to discover what that particular ministry does well. Once these priorities are established, they are to focus on them. The Church can never be all things to all people in one location. Based upon the gifts, the size and the resources, the congregation needs to ascertain what it is they can do within kingdom building that will best suit where they are now. Once the Church establishes priorities, then they can determine not only what they can do but what they cannot do and what they should do now.

A critical aspect of this is to empower the laity. As in the military, the general cannot win the war. The general establishes strategy, but it is the soldiers that actually fight the battle and win the war. In the case of the Church, the Church must empower the laity. It is the lay person that really determines how far ministry goes and grows. The Church will never grow if the pastor or staff is looked upon as getting everything done. The lay person will meet people that the pastor will never meet. So, if they are empowered and encouraged, then ministry really happens. Churches need to reclaim the biblical idea that ministry is not what happens on Sunday morning. Ministry is what happens in the marketplace—where we live, labor, learn and spend our leisure time.

To have ministry happen, we must equip the saints. It is Ephesians 4 that gives us those parameters. The new Christian must be oriented to the bible and to the Christian life. It is not automatic and it is not done by osmosis. One has to learn to be a saint. We are called to be saints but we become saints by learning how to walk in the Word and in the Spirit.

The congregation needs to be constantly admonished that they are change agents in society. We are in the world but not of the world. The Church is to influence the world and not allow the world to influence it. The congregation must be educated to know that we are to focus on the world that is coming, not the world that is going. We are not to love the world (1 John 2:15). Every congregation has strengths and weaknesses, our responsibility is to understand what those weaknesses are and to address them. So these are the areas that make ministry happen. They are called "Helpful Hints to Make Ministry Happen."

- Establish priorities.
- Empower the laity.
- Equip the saints.
- Educate the congregation.
- Elicit help in areas of weakness.

In reality, there are "Hindrances to Ministry".

When one looks at ministries that are not growing, what is usually the problem? Congregations are more organisms than they are organizations. Since organisms are alive, they should grow. Not growing is an indication of disease. What is it that really limits the organism from growing and developing? There are three things that hinder ministry:

- The vision is resisted.
- The voices of members are not heard.
- Victories are not adequately celebrated.

The Book of Proverbs says that where there is no vision, the people perish. Often times the pastor and leadership team understand what it is that God wants them to do, but the congregation has a tendency to resist what they don't understand. As we said earlier, they resist change—because change really means we have to change ourselves. So when the vision of the pastor and the leadership team is resisted, it causes confusion, it causes spiritual delay and it causes a resistance within the congregation. When people don't understand, they tend to do nothing. Vision casting is very important. However, the leader must understand that the starting vision will not be the accepted vision. The vision takes time to develop and patience is necessary in this area.

The pastor has to understand a simple reality: just because God gives the pastor the vision does not automatically mean that the members understand the vision. The voices of the members need to be encouraged and heard. Even if their ideas are not clear, they need to be able to say what they feel, they need to verbalize their reluctance, they need to even articulate their fears. They need to understand their misunderstandings. Even though it takes time, the leadership team must allow the members to buy into the vision. I believe it was John Maxwell who said, "If you are leading and no one is following you, then you are just taking a walk." It is not a waste of time for the leader and leadership team to enlist the members by listening to them and making sure that they understand. They may not always agree, but at least they must be given the opportunity to voice their concerns and even their objections.

The victories that each congregation engages in must be celebrated. Often churches are too concerned about moving to the next project. We often say we want to "take the ministry to the next level." But people need to celebrate the level that they are on, before they are pushed to go to another level. Every year at a special service, every congregation needs to celebrate what God has done in the present year before the church is motivated to take on the task of the next year. Every victory, no matter how large or small, must be celebrated.

You cannot rush into decision making. You cannot just throw a new idea onto the membership. There is a concept called "lag time." This represents the fact that once a vision is cast, the leader must have some built in lag time for the congregation to catch on to the vision. This lag time can be enhanced by teaching, by workshops, by small group sharing, etc. Once the idea is presented, the wise leader will allow weeks and months to pass so that the new idea has the opportunity to germinate in the minds and hearts of the congregation. To lead people by dragging them forward is not real leadership. When the congregation is prepared to lead, then they are more likely to assume responsibility for the vision. Real progress happens when the congregation says it's not only the "pastor's vision" but it is now "our vision." Real progress is being made when one's members are heard saying, "Our vision is to do this or to accomplish that." As long as the members are saying "the pastor's vision," "the pastor's vision", "the pastor's vision", then the vision is neither in their heads nor in their hearts.

How does the pastor get the vision off the paper and into the hearts of the congregation? Again, the pastor must allow some lag time. The pastor must plan, must pray and must proclaim and allow the congregation time to get the vision into their hearts. It's not unusual that one, two or three years into the transition of the church the pastor will continue to hear the members saying, "The pastor's vision." In sharing the vision, the pastor must get the congregation to accept the responsibility to carry the vision out. This must be done first with core leaders. Every church has a core leadership and it is this core leadership that generally is the engine that drives the ministry. Any wise pastor will be certain that the core leaders are onboard before any changes are made. The easiest way for a pastor to lose their congregation and, thus, to lose their job, is to try to make major changes without the support of the core leadership. Although, God gives the pastor the vision, even though the vision is bible based, it is still the human dimension that must carry out the spiritual vision. The wise pastor will make sure that the core leaders are onboard before any major casting of vision is done. In order to share the vision, the pastor moves from getting the core leaders onboard to then getting the extended leaders onboard. In a traditional church, the core leaders might be the ministers, deacons, deaconesses and the lay leaders in the congregation. The extended leaders may be the ministry leaders in the church. When the extended leaders are onboard, we are ready to involve the whole church in the vision. At some point towards the end of the year, meet with the full time staff. Next, meet with all of the general core leaders. Then at the beginning of the new year, meet with all the church. By that time you will have gone over the new steps in the vision three times. You will have had an opportunity to fine tune it. By the time the members hear it, all of the core and extended leaders are onboard. Again, share the vision with core leaders, extended leaders and then the whole church. The clearest way or the easiest way to undermine the vision is to share it with too many people too soon. The key here is to use extended or multiple mediums to share the vision.

Now the process of change can begin. Here again, make one major change at a time. You cannot undermine the entire ministry by changing everything, because members have grown accustomed to the way things are and to upset the congregation with multiple changes, at once, will cause chaos and turmoil and will not bode well. If the church is in need of major change, consider this analogy. If one was going to the hospital and they had a brain tumor, heart disease, liver trouble and bone loss, the surgeon might very well say, "It is not conducive to do surgery at this time, I want to make sure that the patient's body is strong enough to do surgery." If you try to do major surgery in a weak body, you end up killing the body while you try to heal it. Make one major change at a time.

A significant factor is to make sure that you have the right people in the right place. Often churches don't grow because key leadership positions are held by members who are not key and, therefore, they hinder the work of the ministry. As one writer has said, there are five "R's" to succeed in making sure that the right people are in the right place.

- The right person.
- The right place.
- The right reason.
- The right season.
- The right spirit.

If the pastor's spirit is not right or if the leader's spirit is not right, you are going to ruin the chemistry of the ministry. Every ministry needs chemistry in order to go. Look more closely at the five "R's". The right person. You want the person in ministry, that understands that this is the ministry where God really wants him or her to be. One way to tell if one is the right person for a ministry is, do they have passion for that ministry? They use the local expression: When someone is really where God wants them to be, they almost live, eat and sleep that ministry. It does not feel like work to them. They would not want to be anywhere else or doing anything else. That's when you know you have the right person.

The right place simply is that you want the right person in the right place. For example, if someone really loves to work in an office and their job has them climbing telephone poles for the phone company, they might make a lot of money, but over time they are not going to be happy. The same is true in ministry. If someone really has a gift to work in the background and they are encouraged or almost forced to work in a public position, they are not going to be happy. So background persons need to be in the background and those in the public view need to be in the public view. Understand that when one is a background person, it does not mean that they are less important, they just have a different place of ministry.

The right reason. Even leaders must guard against impure motives. You do not want someone in a place because they are supportive, because they are generous givers, because they love the ground that you walk on. You want them there because they are God's man or God's woman for that ministry at that time.

And that's where the right season comes in. There are some who are in the right place this year but may be out of place next year. All of us have seasons of ministry and we can only really bear fruit if we are in the season that God has us prepared for.

The final "R" is the right spirit. One can be the right person, in the right place, for the right reason and the right season, but their spirit is not right, demonstrating a lack of team spirit. There is no place for *"prima donnas"* in ministry. If one's spirit is not right, they're going to ruin the chemistry of the ministry. There's always room in ministry for those who have an "anything it takes" attitude—those who believe that we can get this done, now is the time to do it, and we are the people to get it done. God will always get the job done through those who are right for the job. When God gives you someone to serve as a leader, you have to make sure that you do not allow distractions to get you off track. He says, "I am doing something to you, so that one day I might do something through you." Even when the distractions come, even when discouragement comes, the leader must continue on the path that they are on.

The key in starting the process of change is to make one major change at a time. Make sure people are in the right place. Use the five "R's" and build on your strength.

Expect opposition. I have a saying when it comes to change, we will always encounter opposition—"Opposition—expect it, meet it and beat it." Once you understand that opposition is part of the process, then you will not let it distract or discourage you. The whole study of the Book of Nehemiah is how to fulfill your mission in spite of opposition. One can also expect apathy, anger, criticism and attacks, even personal fights. But here is how the leader must respond: prayer, patience, encouragement and perseverance. Remember, expect opposition, but respond to it in a spiritual way by prayer, patience, encouragement and perseverance. Remind people why changes are being made and then celebrate the successes of the changes that are made.

Once the vision is cast and the members assume responsibility, they must perform what it is they are being asked to do and then have an evaluation of that performance. Every year, each segment of the leadership team must be evaluated. They must understand what they are expected to do and be trained to do it. Leaders must know what they are doing well and what they are not doing well, in order to make the necessary changes that they need to make in order for the ministry to grow.

Developing the Purpose of the Congregation or Developing a Congregation with Purpose

First and foremost, the purpose of the congregation must be Christ's purpose. What was the purpose of Christ's coming to earth? We go right to the Bible to discover this. In Luke 4:18, we read: "The Spirit of the Lord is upon me because He has anointed me to preach the gospel to the poor, he has sent me to heal the brokenhearted, to proclaim liberty to the captives and recovery of sight to the blind, to set at liberty those who are oppressed."

It seems simple enough, but if the Church is not careful, they will be engaged in a ministry that is not the mandate of Christ. The Church can do a lot of things that may be good but are not Christ-centered. How do we know that what we are doing is Christ-centered and how can we tell if our congregation is involved in things that are not? Again, we must seek our direction from the Bible. Ephesians 4 and Leviticus 16 give us the purpose of the Church. We are to engage in the development of the members until they become conformed to the image of Christ. It gives us a clear mandate as to who our target audience is. As a congregation, we are commanded by God to reach the lost, the least, the left out, the lonely, the losers according to society and those who are locked out and knocked down. The Church is not to seek to be a country club but really a hospital. The Church is on target when it communicates the message that none of us are perfect, but we are seeking to become Christ-like and our goal is to share our experiences with others. This attitude says to the community that our ministry is not one of condemnation, but one of invitation. Most people view the Church as being in the ministry of condemnation and not in the ministry of invitation. It is important to note that our Lord Jesus was condemned not for hanging out with priests and rabbis, but he was crucified for hanging out with those that were the outcasts of society. His condemnation actually was a commendation in that he was accused of hanging out with fugitives and sinners. This should be the accusation against every congregation that seeks to be led by the Lord. We should be commended for reaching out to those that are less fortunate, and condemned for only wanting those in our congregation who are up socially acceptable. The purpose must be Christ's purpose and it must be clear. It must be communicated that our ministry is really a "whosoever will, let them come."

Secondly, the purpose of the congregation must be to honor God. Ephesians 4 gives us four commands. We are to walk worthy of our vocation. Since we name Christ and since we are committed to be like Him our lifestyle must reflect the Lordship of Jesus Christ. We are to worship worthily. We are to work worthily, putting on the whole armor of God, (Ephesians 6:11-19). We are to be a worthy witness, fulfilling what the Lord said in the Sermon on the Mount, "Let your light so shine before men, that they may see your good works and glorify your father, which is in heaven."

In summary, the bible is our source of understanding our purpose. The purpose must be to honor God; and the program must promote this purpose. The congregation promotes what they believe by their actions. Doctrine must be connected to duty. We are to say what we believe and then we are to believe what we say. Our belief is not only a covenant that we adhere to, but our belief is a lifestyle that we are committed to. The world needs to see authentic Christians who belong to authentic Churches that do authentic ministry. What is it that we believe? This is known not by what we say, but by what we do. The Church of Jesus Christ must be committed to <u>being</u> more than <u>doing</u>.

Of interest is that our budget reflects what we believe. The church's budget is, in essence, a theological document. If you say you love the seniors, let me see how much they are represented in the budget. If the church is committed to world missions, how much of that is reflected in the budget? If the church believes in education, how much of that is reflected in the budget? The budget becomes a theological document. Two things must be taken into consideration, the church's budget and it's program are to be based on present members. The budget must be promoted to meet the needs of those who are currently in the congregation. The second consideration is that it must also be based on those that you're trying to reach.

The role of the pastor must be honored. The pastor of the congregation must be given the freedom to lead. If at any time a pastor is going to be held accountable for their congregation, then they must be given the freedom to lead that congregation for which they must give account. It is philosophically unfair to have someone in charge and then not give them the freedom to lead. The pastor must be held accountable for leading, but must be given the freedom to lead. They are called to cast the vision and then be given the resources for that vision to become reality.

The pastor must be compensated honorably. It is very difficult to lead a congregation when the pastor's personal package does not reflect the work that they do. Each congregation must be sure that they compensate the pastor in an honorable manner. Based on the budget of that congregation, the minister's financial needs must be met. This is reflected in Galatians 5 and also Jeremiah 3:15 and other supporting passages.

No minister should be allowed the freedom to function without accountability. The life that has no accountability will eventually fail. Pastors must give someone or some group in the congregation the freedom to confront them on their decisions and be given an answer as to why they're doing what they're doing. Any leader that cannot justify his or her actions based on the Word of God should not be followed.

Further, the pastor must be supported with prayer. It is not enough to encourage the pastor financially, but the church must pray for the pastor.

The church must get back to the biblical idea of empowering the people. We must give power back to the people so that the ministry is not personality driven but empowered by the laity. In every major spiritual revival, it has been laity and not clergy that gave it, its impetus. To be clear, it is not to minimize the role of the pastor. The pastor is to function as the spiritual leader of the congregation, but it must be understood that unless the membership is empowered to do ministry, the quality of that ministry will suffer. The task of the clergy, according to Ephesians 4 is to empower the people and equip the people. Each one must reach one and then each one must teach one. The people must accept the responsibility to do the work of ministry.

After empowering and equipping the congregation, we must encourage the people. When we understand that the members have to deal with the daily struggles of life and then engage in ministry, we can understand how easy it is for them to be discouraged. Therefore, the membership must be encouraged by the Word of God, making it possible that the worshiping event not only becomes a saving event but becomes an encouraging event.

The final step is to evaluate the people. Once they are empowered, equipped and encouraged, then they are to be held accountable for the work that they have been assigned to do. This is what really empowers the people—to know their purpose and then, with God's help, to fulfill that purpose.

An important step in the process of preparing your church for change is the time of transition. How do we transition from where the ministry is now, to where we want the ministry to go. The key word in this particular process is tension. Whenever you make changes in any organization's structure, you can understand that tension will be a part of that process. The pastor is the key person in preparing for change. Here are some things you will have to consider.

Prepare for change. What is the present condition of your church? Is your church in a growth spurt? Is your church in a downturn? Has your church reached a plateau? When assessing the conditions for change, the pastor must determine if the members are ready for a paradigm shift. The members must be prepared for change. This is, again, referencing that period of "lag time". From the time the pastor gets the vision to lead his or her church through change, the members must be granted some lag time to understand the vision. Just because God gives the pastor a vision does not mean that the members will automatically be onboard. Thus, the pastor's primary responsibility is to prepare the congregation for change.

Life is always unfinished business but one must accept the need to change in order to make life better. Tension is good when struggling from where you are to where you are going. It is a good thing to have tension in ministry. God is always trying to birth something new. The pastor must understand that the responsibility of casting a vision for change comes from three areas. The pastor must pray and be very clear about where God is leading the church. The pastor must plan. Where are we now? Where are we going? How will we get there? The pastor must proclaim or preach on whatever changes need to be made. In other words, there must be a biblical basis for what the pastor is doing. At this point, in order to make the paradigm shift palatable to the congregation, they must be taught that they are Christian's where they live, labor, and spend their leisure time. Most churches plateau or decline because they forget that Christianity is not a Sunday only dynamic. The Church must be constantly challenged to live out faith. This will create tension. Most Christians are comfortable where they are and are not always amenable to the challenge of change or being confronted. This is why the pastor must pray much, plan much and proclaim much before the change is implemented.

Examine the condition of the church and the concerns of the membership. What are the members' concerns? What are they really interested in accomplishing? Experience shows us that most members are concerned primarily about two groups. One being the youth and the other the senior members. Any real change must always take into consideration those who are coming along and those who have been in the congregation for some time. For instance, if you are in an area where there is a change in the makeup of that community from a traditionally European settled community to an African American, Latino or Asian community, then your church has to be prepared to reach out to those who are racially and ethnically different.

Consider the level of commitment of the laity in your congregation. The laity must be committed. The laity is defined as non clergy or non ordained persons. The commitment of the laity is germane for any change, for the laity are those who will make it happen.

Next in preparing for change is a call to biblical discipleship. Membership is not the intent of Christianity, it is discipleship. Jesus says in Matthew 28:18-20 that we are to go into all the world and make disciples, students, learners, pupils, those who really want to know how to live the Christian life.

Finally, in preparing for change, our purpose must be to honor God. Church growth is not about making a celebrity out of the pastor. Church growth is not about becoming a mega church. Church growth is about honoring God. The pastor and people must both be committed to honoring God. So the pastor must again, pray, plan and proclaim the change that God is leading him to make and the church must be prepared for change. Change is not automatic and change must undergo the resistance or the tension that comes from the fact that objects that are static seek to remain static. Churches that are not growing or have not been challenged will resist change, even though the change may be for their benefit.

The pastor should be able to define the vision in one sentence. What is it that God is leading you to lead the church to do? Part of defining the vision is to discover your purpose, what to do? If the church is going through a downturn in membership or if the community is going through transition, then often the church must go back and rediscover their purpose. In other words the church needs to remember why it was birthed in the first place. What is the reason that the church was placed into existence by the Lord. In Matthew, Chapter 16, Jesus says, "Upon this rock I will build my church and the gates of hell will not prevail against it." Our purpose is to build or develop a community of faith, that can live out the mission of Christ in the world. That is the purpose of the church.

In defining your vision you define your target group. Who will do what? Someone has said that if you aim at nothing, you will hit it every time. Although the church is called to reach everyone, oftentimes because of the church's location there may be a particular target group whose needs the church will want to meet.

The leadership should agree on a strategy. How will change be implemented? In defining your vision, you first must know your purpose, what to do? Then identify your target group, who will do it? And finally, decide your strategy, how to do it? In this case, every aspect of the ministry must be evaluated and those things that are not working must be discarded. We have often heard that the last seven words of a dying church is, "We've never done it that way before." Members must be challenged to understand that if the church does not go through changes, not change for the sake of change but change to meet the generation that it is in now and the generation that is coming, then that church will be out of business.

Many churches do not understand that each year thousands of congregations literally close their doors. When the Lord says in Matthew 16 that the church will prevail, he's not talking about your church or my church, he's talking about His church. So the only church that has the authority of heaven behind it and the power of God within it is the church that is His by ownership. Christ must be the head of the church if He is expected to grow the church. The key here is—to be dynamic, you must be specific. What to do? Who will do it? How to do it? And to have some kind of evaluation process in place.

The pastor is now ready to plant the vision. Here the leader must secure the support that is needed. In order to cast a vision, the pastor must have the support of more than a simple majority in the congregation. By praying, planning and proclaiming, the pastor can gain the support that is needed in order to grow the church. Again, no one can do the work of ministry alone. God gives gifts to every member that they may use them to help build up the Body of

Christ, as we discussed in Ephesians 4. After the pastor secures the support that is needed, he or she must labor to secure the assistance that is needed. The pastor must identify individuals who will take responsibility for the work. This is crucial because the church is a volunteer organization. Even though a ministry might have several paid staff, the paid staff cannot grow the church. It is still incumbent upon the laity, or the volunteers to put in place the changes that the pastor has in mind.

The next step is to secure the advice you need. In ministering, one need not reinvent the wheel. If there is another ministry that is doing what God is leading you to do, then the pastor and/or leaders might visit that particular church site and meet with that leader. In our congregation, we took 25 leaders from San Mateo, California to Little Rock, Arkansas to visit St. Mark's Baptist Church. We spent several days shadowing their leaders and meeting with the pastor. It was one of the major influences that helped our church to grow. Often people walk by sight, when they really should walk by faith. But the reality is, seeing is believing for some people. Often, if your congregation can see a model of what you're trying to do, it might gain the assistance and support needed for your ministry. The key here is to expose your leaders to other models and ministry "best practices".

The Four Dimensions
of a Complete Life

The optimum word for life and ministry is balance. The balanced life is a blessed one. The life that is out of balance will breed harmful and unhealthy patterns. The people of God as with all people tend to struggle with balance. We tend to error on the side of hyper spirituality or base carnality or some gray zone in between. In my pastoral ministry, I have noticed at least four areas that need balance in order for life to have a sense of completeness. They are spiritual, physical, relational and financial. In many minority communities, the local church must meet a myriad of needs. Whereas a suburban congregation may have access to the essentials for a high quality of life, it is not normative for urban ministries. The key for every ministry is to have intentionality.

Spiritual

The congregation must rest on a spiritual foundation. It may be assumed that this is a given but not so. Many congregations are experiencing a modern day wilderness journey. When Moses was leading the people out of bondage, they were unhappy campers for the most part. (Exodus 14:11-15) Little has changed. Congregations must determine whether it is going to engage in business as usual or unusual business.

Physical

The people of God can be out of shape physically. In the African-American community the highest incidence of most illnesses are found. A program of health education is necessary. The theology of health and wholeness is often missing in their ministry. Fortunately, this is changing. If the body is sick then the ministry is going to be adversely affected.

Relational

The congregation is made of many relationships. I have said in sermons that whoever you are in the parking lot is who you are in the worship center. The people that make up our parishes usually come to us with some degree of dysfunction. Several years ago, we added a licensed family therapist to our staff. The difference that the therapist has made is remarkable. However, it is surprising that many people are unwilling to address their interpersonal issues.

Financial

One of the sobering statistics of most churches is the number of members who give little or nothing to their ministries. Most leaders are unaware of the paucity of their stewardship component. It is not uncommon for as little as ten percent of the congregation to carry ninety percent of the financial burden for the church. A yearly evaluation of the congregation's giving pattern is the means of solving this problem. Most ministries lose their vitality because of a lack of funds.

See figures 1-5 (PDF-Four Dimensions)

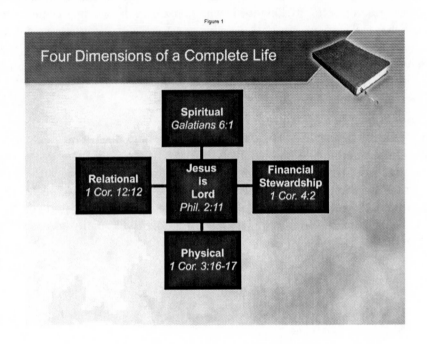

Figure 1

Four Dimensions of a Complete Life

Figure 2

Spiritual *Galatians 6:1*

- Taking responsibility for your "God" connection

- Covering your Brothers and Sisters

- Ministry of Restoration

- The Church is God's "Hospital"

Figure 3

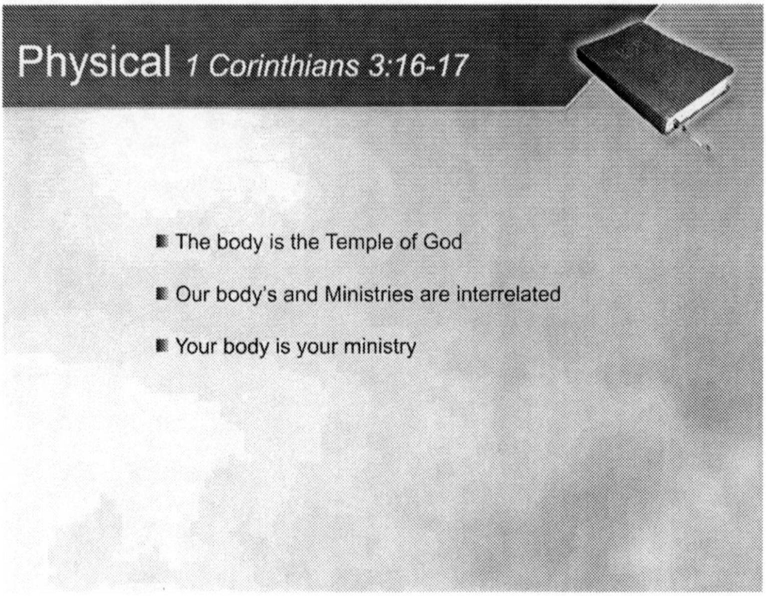

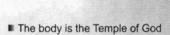

Physical *1 Corinthians 3:16-17*

- The body is the Temple of God
- Our body's and Ministries are interrelated
- Your body is your ministry

Figure 4

Relational *1 Corinthians 12:12*

Develop healthy relationships in the Church Body the *5 R's*:

- right *Person*
- right *Place*
- right *Season*
- right *Reason*
- right *Spirit*

Figure 5

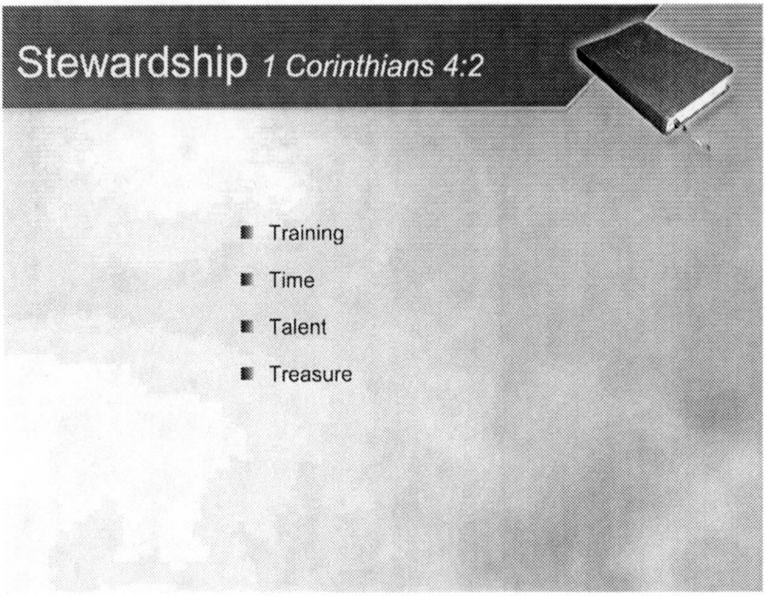

Stewardship *1 Corinthians 4:2*

- Training
- Time
- Talent
- Treasure

The Vision

Many pastors and churches have adopted a vision statement from other ministries without thinking them through. Although there is no need to reinvent the wheel, some prayer and thought must go into casting the vision for your ministry. I have discovered that the pastor must teach and preach on the vision before implementing it. Moreover, some time must be given for the membership to absorb the new direction that the Lord is leading. Conflict can be minimized or avoided all together by allowing what I refer to as "lag time", that is the time between the leader getting the vision and the congregation getting it. The prophet Habakkuk was told to write the vision that the people of God may read it and then run with it or simply put carry it out.(Habakkuk 2:1-3) The writer of Proverbs (29:18) states that without vision the people will perish. It may be that many congregations of all faiths are failing to flourish because there is no agreed upon vision statement. Jesus' pronouncement of the promise found in Matthew 16:13-18, that the gates of hell will not prevail against his church, has lulled many believers into a false sense of security. The Lord will keep the work going, is their sentiment as He has promised. How then, would one explain the large number of churches that close each year and the new church plants that never come into fruition? The next function of vision is to communicate how the vision will benefit the congregation. The "what is in it for me" syndrome applies to believers also. The parents of children who are a few years from college age will support the part of the vision that will provide education assistance. The adult children of elderly parents will support the part of the vision that includes senior housing. However, the ministry must have a kingdom component or it may be self-serving as well as self centered. (See Acts 2:41-47 and Second Cor.9:15) The last piece of the vision is achieving victory. The two components of victory are equal sacrifice (second Cor. 2:6) and equal service (Phil. 3:13-16). There is no greater joy than for ministry to dream, design and deliver on a project. It builds both momentum for the present and motivation for the next phase of ministry. I have used a simple formula that has aided me in serving one congregation for twenty years. 1) projects take longer than expected. 2) Projects always cost more than expected. 3) Projects have more obstacles than expected.

The Desired Outcome

1. Every member in Sunday School/Home Bible Study/Serving in Ministry.

2. Every ministry has an outreach component.

3. Every member will become a tither.

4. Every member will have their needs met through Christian love.

5. Every member accountable to one another.

6. Every member using their gift in ministry.

See figures 6-14 (PDF-Congregation Driven)

Figure 6

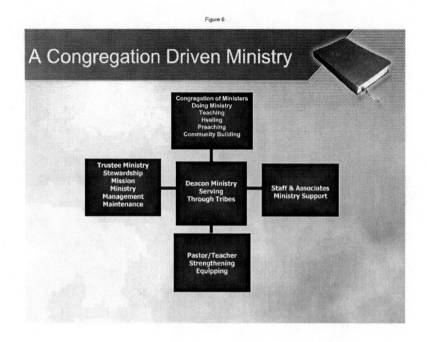

Figure 7

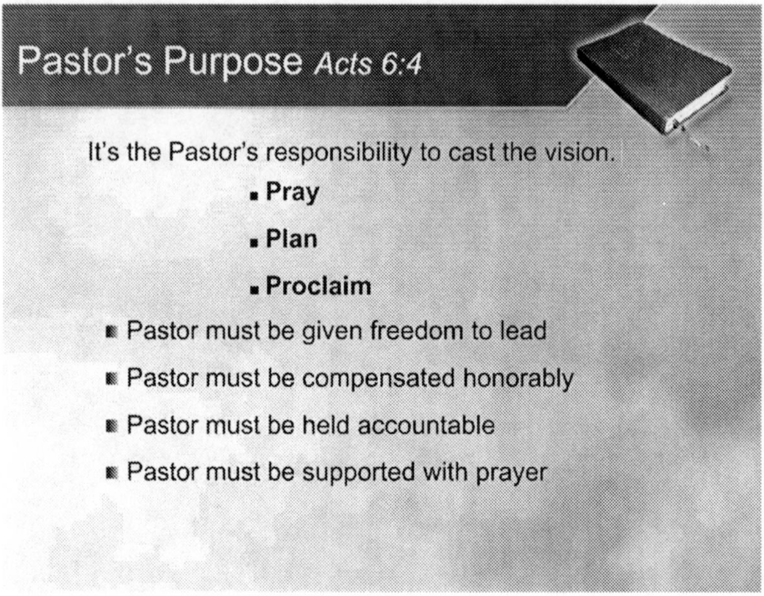

Pastor's Purpose *Acts 6:4*

It's the Pastor's responsibility to cast the vision.
- **Pray**
- **Plan**
- **Proclaim**
- Pastor must be given freedom to lead
- Pastor must be compensated honorably
- Pastor must be held accountable
- Pastor must be supported with prayer

Figure 8

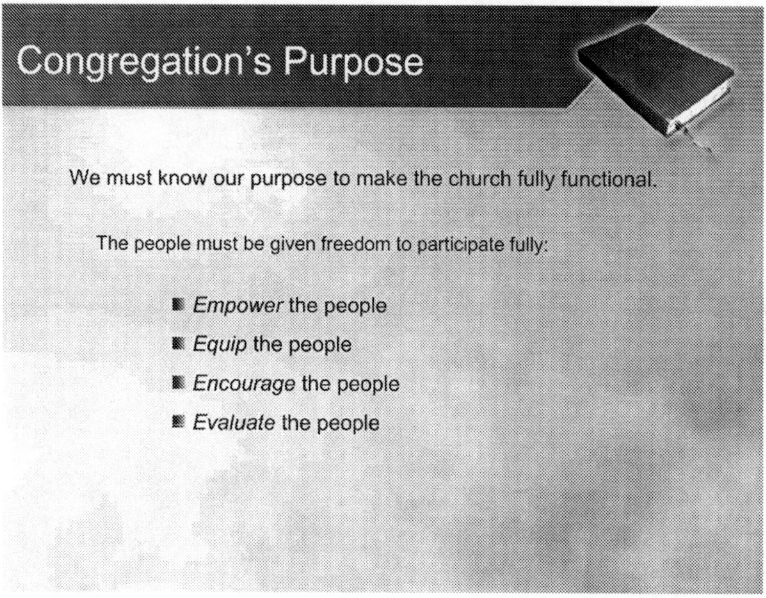

Congregation's Purpose

We must know our purpose to make the church fully functional.

The people must be given freedom to participate fully:

- *Empower* the people
- *Equip* the people
- *Encourage* the people
- *Evaluate* the people

Figure 9

Deacons Support

- Pastor's Vision
- Caring for the Congregation
- Fulfilling *Acts 6:1-6*
- Working the Tribal System

Figure 10

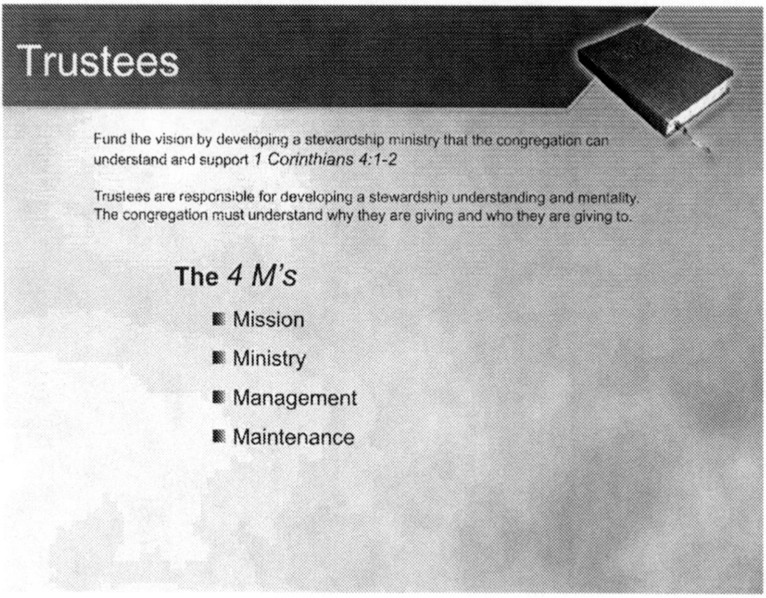

Trustees

Fund the vision by developing a stewardship ministry that the congregation can understand and support *1 Corinthians 4:1-2*

Trustees are responsible for developing a stewardship understanding and mentality. The congregation must understand why they are giving and who they are giving to.

The *4 M's*

- Mission
- Ministry
- Management
- Maintenance

Figure 11

Church Staff

- Promotes the vision given by the Pastor.

- Works together to promote the vision.

- Making sure that the vision is integrated into the life of the Church.

Figure 12

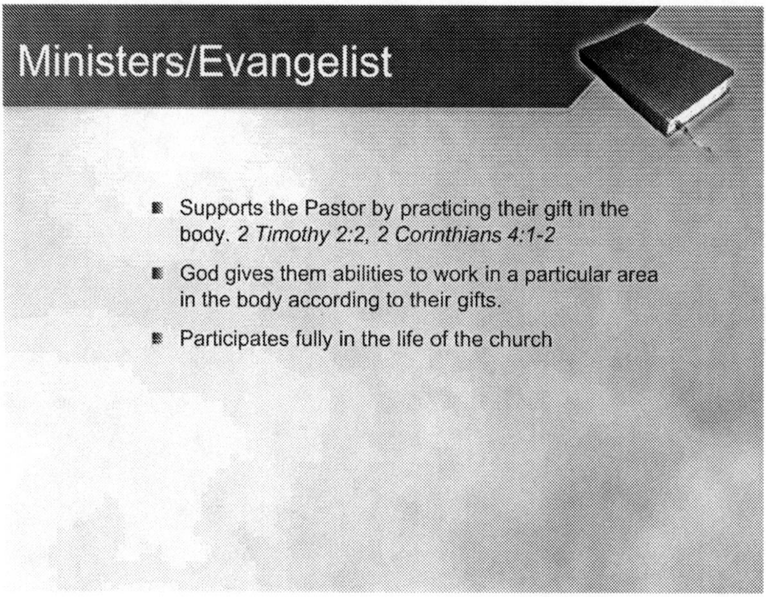

Ministers/Evangelist

- Supports the Pastor by practicing their gift in the body. *2 Timothy 2:2, 2 Corinthians 4:1-2*

- God gives them abilities to work in a particular area in the body according to their gifts.

- Participates fully in the life of the church

Figure 13

Congregation Commitment

Acts 2:42-47

- to Christ
- to the Church
- to the word of God
- to following the Pastor's vision
- to the use of spiritual gifts in ministry

Figure 14

Stages of Growth

Moving from Membership to Maturity:

■ Salvation

■ Preparation

■ Responsibility

■ Evaluation

Part 1

Acts 8:1-8

1. Persecution can lead to Promotion:

    a. Christians can get in a comfort zone

    b. Churches can get in a comfort zone

    c. Christ sends conflict to get us out of our comfort zone

2. Preach in spite of Problems:

    a. Preachers stayed

    b. People scattered

    c. Preached sermon

3. Purpose is to reach People:

    a. People need help

    b. People need to hear

    c. People need healing

4. Every pastor has the responsibility of leading the church to fulfill the great commission of Jesus Christ.

Conclusion: The Joy of Salvation

Matthew 28:18-20
And Jesus came and spake unto them, saying, All power is given unto me in heaven and in earth. [19] Go ye therefore, and teach all nations, baptizing them in the name of the Father, and of the Son, and of the Holy Ghost: [20] Teaching them to observe all things whatsoever I have commanded you: and, lo, I am with you alway, even unto the end of the world. Amen.

The pastor must search the Scriptures to understand the word, will and way that God would lead the particular church to do ministry. Christian ministry does not just happen. Many churches die or close their doors because they feel that even if they do nothing, Jesus will keep the doors open.

Matthew 16:18
And I say also unto thee, That thou art Peter, and upon this rock I will build my church; and the gates of hell shall not prevail against it.

We began to implement a ministry model called The Congregation Driven Ministry ten years ago. It is based on several Scriptures. The pastor's role is to teach the membership to take the lead in doing ministry.

Ephesians 4: 11-12
And he gave some, apostles; and some, prophets; and some, evangelists; and some, pastors and teachers; [12] For the perfecting of the saints, for the work of the ministry, for the edifying of the body of Christ:

Members must know Christ for themselves. They must discover their own spiritual gifts and get involved in ministry. It is not the role of the pastor alone to reach those who do not know Christ. The pastor's role is to train the members to share Christ where they live, labor, learn and spend their leisure time. The church must put ministries in place to assist the members to mature in their faith and get involved in Christian ministry.

In our text, the first church is experiencing intense persecution. A young man from Tarsus named Saul is ravaging the young church. Why has the Lord Jesus allowed this young fellowship to go through such severe testing? He said the gates of hell would not win over them, why this? Why now? The church is guilty of a serious sin. They have entered a comfort zone. Maybe you were going through a difficult time, you asked the Lord to make a way for you, and he did. You were so committed to the church. You loved Bible study and enjoyed serving others. After sometime you began to cool off. When God blesses us he takes a chance on losing us. Some Christians can handle problems better than prosperity. I believe this is the case in the early church. Peter's first sermon brings five thousand to the church. The second message adds another three thousand. Success can spoil you if you do not stay rooted and grounded in God. Let us look at what happen:

> But ye shall receive power, after that the Holy Ghost is come upon you: and ye shall be witnesses unto me both in Jerusalem, and in all Judaea, and in Samaria, and unto the uttermost part of the earth.

- Acts 1(mission) Acts 1:8
- Acts 2 (miracle) Pentecost
- Acts 3 (ministry) healed the paralyzed man
- Acts 4 (message)
- Acts 5 (money) Ananias and Sapphira
- Acts 6 (meal) widows
- Acts 7 (murder of Stephen)
- Acts 8 (misery)

The church had become stationary and no longer missionary. Instead of standing on the promises, they were just sitting on the premises. Churches as well as individuals can get satisfied with their success. It is not a sin to have success but it is a sin to let success get in the way of service.

The church is at ease may be resting on their laurels. Jesus told them to go into all the world. They have stopped in Jerusalem. He said, Jerusalem, Judea, Samaria and the entire world. Jesus rose up Saul to stir up the church. The Lord will comfort the afflicted and afflict the comfortable. Stephen, a great deacon was picked out to be picked on. When the church stands still, members can be picked off. Stephen was stoned to death. He was filled with the Holy Ghost yet he was stoned. He was a student of the word, yet he was stoned. Sometimes bad things happen to good people. When something bad happens to someone, it may be that they are doing something right and not something wrong.

The church is scattered. This is an interesting word. It means to be sown as seed. The church would not go out on its own, so God permitted Saul to chase them out to the mission field. It is always best to obey God by choice than to be forced to obey by circumstances.

The Apostles stayed in Jerusalem. It was not the preachers who were to go out and spread the word it was the members. It showed courage and stability to hold down the church in the midst of death and danger.

The people scattered to places God sent them. As they went from one place to another, they preached. It took the problem of persecution to get them to preach. It took the murder of Stephen to get the people to move out. It took wounding them to get them to worship. The church was on the run. They got their priorities right while they were persecuted.

- Some people have problems and stay at home.
- Some people lose their job and stay at home.
- Some people have trouble in their home and stay at home.
- Some people face tragedy and stay at home.

The child of God should continue praising God in spite of their problems. Christians are made to soar and not sit.

The purpose of the church is to reach people. Jesus loves people. He was born to save people. He lived to serve people. He did miracles to help people. The church of Jesus Christ is to do what He did. He loves all people but he has a special place in his heart for sinners, those of us who know that we need Him in our lives.

Saul consented to the death of Deacon Stephen, but God raised up another deacon—Philip. Deacons are so important in The Congregation Driven Ministry. They are examples of servanthood. Deacon Philip went to Samaria. He went to those who needed and wanted to help.

- The least
- The lonely
- The left out
- The let down
- The locked up
- The locked down

Philip preached Christ.

John 3:16-19
For God so loved the world, that he gave his only begotten Son, that whoso-ever believeth in him should not perish, but have everlasting life. [17] For God sent not his Son into the world to condemn the world; but that the world through him might be saved. [18] He that believeth on him is not con-demned: but he that believeth not is condemned already, because he hath not believed in the name of the only begotten Son of God. [19] And this is the condemnation, that light is come into the world, and men loved darkness rather than light, because their deeds were evil.

 - The spiritually needy heard him.
 - The physically needy heard him.

Acts 8:7
For unclean spirits, crying with loud voice, came out of many that were pos-sessed with them: and many taken with palsies, and that were lame, were healed.

He, a deacon performed the same ministry as Jesus.

Luke 4:18-19
The Spirit of the Lord is upon me, because he hath anointed me to preach the gospel to the poor; he hath sent me to heal the brokenhearted, to preach deliv-erance to the captives, and recovering of sight to the blind, to set at liberty them that are bruised, [19] To preach the acceptable year of the Lord.

God used persecution, to teach that lives are changed by any person who will live a Spirit filled life. It is not based on title, gender, age or knowledge. If every mem-ber will take the initiative to know Christ, know his word, walk in his Spirit they can do what Deacon Philip did! The congregation preached. The congregation taught. The congregation cast out unclean spirits. The congregation healed the sick. It happened then and it can happen again.

Acts 8:8
And there was great joy in that city.

Luke 15:1-7
They drew near unto him all the publicans and sinners for to hear him. [2] And the Pharisees and scribes murmured, saying, This man receiveth sinners,

and eateth with them. [3] And he spake this parable unto them, saying, [4] What man of you, having an hundred sheep, if he lose one of them, doth not leave the ninety and nine in the wilderness, and go after that which is lost, until he find it? [5] And when he hath found it, he layeth it on his shoulders, rejoicing. [6] And when he cometh home, he calleth together his friends and neighbors, saying unto them, Rejoice with me; for I have found my sheep which was lost. [7] I say unto you, that likewise joy shall be in heaven over one sinner that repenteth, more than over ninety and nine just persons, which need no repentance.

- Joy when the lost are saved.
- Joy when the unchurched find a home.
- Joy when the sick are healed.
- Joy when the possessed are delivered.
- Joy that is unspeakable.
- Joy that the world cannot give and the world cannot take away!

Part 2

Acts 11:19-26

1. Encounter:

   a. Persecution

   b. Preaching (Romans 1:16)

   c. Privilege (Suffer)

2. Experience:

   a. Grace

   b. Gladness (gratitude)

   c. Growth

3. Evangelistic:

   a. Reached out (lost)

   b. Reached back (Saul)

   c. Reached within (unsaved member)

4. Drop your bucket where you are

Conclusion: In Christ

The office of education informs us that thirty-three percent (33%) of the students entering the ninth grade do not graduate from high school. When a student enters high school and fails to finish we refer to them as dropouts.

A dropout is anyone who abandons a chosen path. One who withdraws from a membership based upon inactivity or non-involvement. I am interested in this dropout concept because I believe that we find a parallel in the church of Jesus Christ. For many who enter the fellowship and place their names on the church roll fail to graduate to discipleship or spiritual maturity. They may be present on Sunday morning, usually late, but never reach a place where they are willing and able to share their faith with someone who does not know the Lord. The vision of The Congregation Driven Ministry is a bible-based vision of every member involved in ministry. The tribal concept is a means of decreasing dropouts. It is not the role of the pastor to make you grow. It is the goal of the pastor to equip every member for ministry. If we embrace the tribal concept there will be few dropouts.

Ephesians 4: 11-16
And he gave some, apostles; and some, prophets; and some, evangelists; and some, pastors and teachers; [12] For the perfecting of the saints, for the work of the ministry, for the edifying of the body of Christ: [13] Till we all come in the unity of the faith, and of the knowledge of the Son of God, unto a perfect man, unto the measure of the stature of the fullness of Christ: [14] That we henceforth be no more children, tossed to and fro, and carried about with every wind of doctrine, by the sleight of men, and cunning craftiness, whereby they lie in wait to deceive; [15] But speaking the truth in love, may grow up into him in all things, which is the head, even Christ: [16] From whom the whole body fitly joined together and compacted by that which every joint supplieth, according to the effectual working in the measure of every part, maketh increase of the body unto the edifying of itself in love.

In chapter eight, we read that Saul of Tarsus, stirred up persecution in the church that led to the murder of Stephen, one of the first deacons. The Apostles stayed in Jerusalem. However, the rest of the believers were scattered to Judea and Samaria to preach the gospel. What God could not get the church to do voluntarily, he accomplished through persecution. It is far better to obey God freely than for God to make us obey by sending trials and trouble. In The Congregation Driven Ministry, every member is a minister. A minister is a servant. If your ministry takes place only in a building, then you have no ministry.

Matthew 28:18-20
And Jesus came and spake unto them, saying, All power is given unto me in heaven and in earth. [19] Go ye therefore, and teach all nations, baptizing them in the name of the Father, and of the Son, and of the Holy Ghost: [20] Teaching them to observe all things whatsoever I have commanded you: and, lo, I am with you alway, even unto the end of the world. Amen.

Each believer is called to stand on the promises, not just sit on the premises. We are to be missionary and not stationary. I am moved by this text because in it we find the disciples referred to as Christians. Something was going on in the city of Antioch that led the people to refer to the members of that congregation as Christian or belonging to Christ. Even though they were scattered by persecution they did not dropout. Today's church will never be able to turn the world upside down or right side up as this church did until we recover authentic Christianity. Maya Angelou was commenting on this when she met a group of people who had just accepted Christ and they were boasting that they were good Christians. She replied "already". Christian is what others see in you, not just a name you go by. Christianity is a life style. You remember the Milli-Vanilli? They were burning up the record charts until it was discovered that they were lip synchronizing and not singing. If we are not careful, we will lip synch the Christian life and not truly live the Christian life!

ENCOUNTER

When the members were scattered by Saul and other persecutors they sowed the good seed of the gospel. They preached Christ. They moved from their comfort zone to share their faith.

When they preached, they preached to Jews only, Acts 11:19

Now they which were scattered abroad, upon the persecution that arose about Stephen traveled as far as Phenice, Cyprus, and Antioch, preaching the word to none but unto the Jews only.

When they got out of their comfort zone, they were ready for the next level of revelation. It was this—that the gospel was not for Jews only. It is for whosoever believes. Now, we have to relearn this basic truth all over again. The gospel does not discriminate. God is Spirit and they that worship him must worship him in Spirit. God does not have a color and we cannot make him in any color or image. That is idolatry! Authentic Christians preach Christ and him crucified. When you encounter Christ, it is a privilege to know him. It is a privilege to be a child of God. It is a privilege to be saved. It is a privilege to tell someone of God's love. How can we feel his love and saving power and not tell everybody about him. The truth is that you do not have to learn to witness. A baby does not take a class in crying. When they want you to know something, they fill their lungs with air and cry. When God has been good to you, your soul is filled with joy and you testify.

EXPERIENCE

When the church was willing to preach to anyone, anytime and anywhere, then God moved. God will only bless a stuck church just so much. God will bless a segregated church just so much.

Acts 11:21
And the hand of the Lord was with them: and a great number believed, and turned unto the Lord.

- The hand of the Lord with them … that's anointing
- A great number believed … that's salvation
- They turned to the Lord … that's commitment

The mother church in Jerusalem heard about what God was doing and they sent Barnabas to evaluate it. Is it real? Are they sincere?

Barnabas saw the grace of God. (verse 22)

Barnabas saw Christian's not just attenders (Rick Warren)

- Attenders just show up on Sunday … Christians commit to ministry.
- Attenders are spectators from the sidelines … Christians get involved.
- Attenders consume ministry … Christians contribute to ministry.
- Attenders just want the church's benefits … Christians share the responsibilities.

Barnabas saw gladness in the church.

- They loved one another.
- They bore one another's burdens.

- They prayed for one another.
- They put up with one another's quirks and idiosyncrasies.
- Christ was the head of the church.
- They had joy, even in the midst of difficulties. They were glad to be in bible study. Small groups met in homes. Will you join one of our home bible studies?

Barnabas saw growth in the church.

Acts 11:24
For he was a good man, and full of the Holy Ghost and of faith: and much people was added unto the Lord.

The church grows as a result of Christians doing what Jesus did. He ministered to the lost, the least, the let down and the left out. We cannot be exclusive. We must be inclusive. God will judge us based upon how we treat those outside of church.

Matthew 25:31-40
When the Son of man shall come in his glory, and all the holy angels with him, then shall he sit upon the throne of his glory: [32] And before him shall be gathered all nations: and he shall separate them one from another, as a shepherd divideth his sheep from the goats: [33] And he shall set the sheep on his right hand, but the goats on the left. [34] Then shall the King say unto them on his right hand, Come, ye blessed of my Father, inherit the kingdom prepared for you from the foundation of the world: [35] For I was an hungred, and ye gave me meat: I was thirsty, and ye gave me drink: I was a stranger, and ye took me in: [36] Naked, and ye clothed me: I was sick, and ye visited me: I was in prison, and ye came unto me. [37] Then shall the righteous answer him, saying, Lord, when saw we thee an hungred, and fed thee? or thirsty, and gave thee drink? [38] When saw we thee a stranger, and took thee in? or naked, and clothed thee? [39] Or when saw we thee sick, or in prison, and came unto thee? [40] And the King shall answer and say unto them, Verily I say unto you, Inasmuch as ye have done it unto one of the least of these my brethren, ye have done it unto me.

EVANGELISTIC

Barnabas saw the grace of God. He witnessed gladness in the lives of the saints. He also saw a growing church. Why were they called by the wonderful name of Christ?

They reached out.

Proverbs 11:30
The fruit of the righteous is a tree of life; and he that winneth souls is wise. It is a mark of authentic Christianity when you seek opportunities to tell others of your faith. We all know of persons in our families, in our schools, on our jobs, even neighbors who need Christ in their lives. It is not your place to try to change anyone but you can tell of God's goodness to you.

They reached back. Barnabas went to find Saul. Saul had wreaked havoc in their church. Saul had consented to Stephen's death but they sent for him. Maybe we need to reach back to those people that we used to sin with and lead them to Christ. Maybe we need to witness to our past partners and bring them to God. They also reached within. Many people are coming to church seeking a relationship with God. We need to minister to those who may be in church but not in Christ. They were called Christians in Antioch because they reached out, back and within. As Christians, we must stop finding our pleasure in the things of this world. We must strive to lift up the name of Jesus. Build up your church. Encourage your leaders. Love your pastor. Praise your ministry leader.

ILLUSTRATION

The story is told of a ship that had been in the midst of one storm after another. The captain and crew were at the point of dying of thirst. The captain saw a ship in the far distance and sent out a frantic SOS. We are dying of thirst, send water. The ship responded, drop your buckets where you are. The captain sent another SOS, we are about to die send water. Again the response, drop your buckets where you are. One last time the captain said ... dying of thirst send water. Again, drop your buckets where you are. The captain dropped the buckets and found that they were in fresh water. It was the Amazon river.

- When you find Christ ... drop your bucket.
- When you find a bible church ... drop your bucket.
- I found him and I dropped my bucket.

- Who can remove your pain?
- Who alone can remove your shame?
- Who can turn the tide in your favor?
- Christ that is who! He will never leave you nor forsake you.
- He died for you. He rose for you.
- He makes intercession for you. He loves you. Drop your bucket in Christ!

Part 3

No One Left Behind

Joshua 1:1-11

1. The People:

    a. all pass over

    b. all possess land

    c. all prosper

2. The Plan:

    a. stay in his word

    b. stay in his will

    c. stay with us

3. The Promise:

    a. presence

    b. power

    c. provision

PRINCIPLE IN ACTION

Mark 6:31-42

If I discovered gold and wanted every member to share the wealth, I would have a difficult time contacting every member. It would not matter which day of the week I invited you to come hear the good news some members would never get the message of their potential wealth! The church is in the midst of tsunami like change. Just like the winds of Hurricane Katrina and Rita, the winds of change are blowing through the church. Mega churches and their bishops headline the news with multi-million dollar budgets and campus facilities, but they are not the majority. Most churches are near death, especially California congregations. The reason most churches are declining in growth, is because of their resistance to change. The average member does not recognize their importance to the well being of the church. A small percentage of the congregation carries on the real ministry of the church.

Matthew 16:17-18
And Jesus answered and said unto him, Blessed art thou, Simon Barjona: for flesh and blood hath not revealed it unto thee, but my Father which is in heaven. [18] And I say also unto thee, That thou art Peter, and upon this rock I will build my church; and the gates of hell shall not prevail against it.

When Jesus spoke, he was not guaranteeing the preservation of every church. We know that this is true because every year thousands of churches close their doors. Each pastor has the God given responsibility to cast a vision for the people that God has called the pastor to serve. The congregation has divine accountability to receive the vision and work diligently to carry it out to the glory of God. The Congregation Driven Ministry is our church's model. It is a spiritual gold mine. It is Christ centered and bible based. It is scriptural at its core. It is the belief that every member is a minister i.e., a servant. The design is to enable each member to grow to become a fully functioning person in the body. When the church functions according to scripture each person has the opportunity to use their gift in ministry and grow to maturity. It is God's desire and mine that no member is left behind in his or her spiritual development. After years of study and working on this concept, it is clear to me that the deacons cannot make the ministry work by themselves. One person cannot minister to the needs of fifty others. One year ago while studying the Old Testament, I came across the tribe system and the light came on. The natural outgrowth of The Congregation Driven Ministry is to organize the church in tribes for accountability and caring. In this God ordained concept no one is left behind.

The book of Joshua opens with the death of Moses. Moses is a great leader and he is never forgotten. He is mentioned dozens of time in the book after his death. Warren Wiersbe writes in "Be Strong" that God buries his workers but never his work.

The work goes on. Joshua is told to lead the people. He has been a spiritual understudy for forty years. God gives him the commission to lead the people.

Leadership requires:

1. Commission

   True leaders are called by God, they do not just volunteer. They are commissioned.

2. Courage

   It takes courage to lead. God tells Joshua to be strong. A weak leader is more interested in pleasing people than God. It is said that if you please everybody and fail to please God you are a failure. If you please God and no one else you are a success.

3. Commitment

   The committed person does not serve when it is convenient. They order their lives around God. He is not an after thought. Christians cannot be satisfied giving God leftovers: leftover time, leftover talent, leftover tithe which is not a tithe at all. Some people still say they do not understand tithing. It is giving God ten percent (10%) of your gross income.

THE PEOPLE

God gave Joshua the command to take all of the people into the Promised Land. No one is to be left behind.

- All pass over.
- All possess land.
- All prosper.

Joshua is leading a new generation into new territory. Each tribe is responsible to lead their tribe. Joshua could not be responsible for two million people.

There were twelve tribe leaders and within the tribe there were leaders of thousands, hundreds and fifties. Every tribe would have an inheritance. Every family would prosper. Every person had to participate. The current occupants of the land did not receive an eviction notice. They were not going to leave without a fight. God has given us every spiritual gift but the flesh will not give in without a fight. God has made us the head and not the tail, but Satan will not give up without a fight. They were in a war and so are we. Listen to Paul …

Ephesians 6:11-19
Put on the whole armour of God, that ye may be able to stand against the wiles of the devil. [12] For we wrestle not against flesh and blood, but against principalities, against powers, against the rulers of the darkness of this world, against spiritual wickedness in high places. [13] Wherefore take unto you the whole armour of God, that ye may be able to withstand in the evil day, and having done all, to stand. [14] Stand therefore, having your loins girt about with truth, and having on the breastplate of righteousness; [15] And your feet shod with the preparation of the gospel of peace; [16] Above all, taking the shield of faith, wherewith ye shall be able to quench all the fiery darts of the wicked. [17] And take the helmet of salvation, and the sword of the Spirit, which is the word of God: [18] Praying always with all prayer and supplication in the Spirit, and watching thereunto with all perseverance and supplication for all saints; [19] And for me, that utterance may be given unto me, that I may open my mouth boldly, to make known the mystery of the gospel.

In our plan, every member is called to belong not just believe (Rick Warren). If we think of the tribes as small units of church within the church, interconnected and dependent to one another. Church membership requires that each of us commit to the advancement of others and not please ourselves. We need to belong to something larger than ourselves. The church is eternal and will be forever. Your membership in the church is the highest membership you will ever belong to. In this system, the Lord promised prosperity. It means that each member's needs are met so that no one is left out or left behind.

Consider that twenty percent of the members give over one half of the church's income. If one-half of all working members gave ten percent it would triple our budget.

- Every student would able to attend any college.
- Every senior would be assisted with housing and medicine.
- Pilgrim Organization, Inc. could develop jobs for unemployed members.

- Members who became unemployed could be helped for several months.

We could do all of this and more if every member committed to give both money and ministry.

THE PLAN

This plan was put in place by God and was never revoked. It worked then and it will work today. When I look at the newspaper the word of God to Hosea comes to mind.

Hosea 4:1-6
Hear the word of the Lord, ye children of Israel: for the Lord hath a controversy with the inhabitants of the land, because there is no truth, nor mercy, nor knowledge of God in the land. [2] By swearing, and lying, and killing, and stealing, and committing adultery, they break out, and blood toucheth blood. [3] Therefore shall the land mourn, and every one that dwelleth therein shall languish, with the beasts of the field, and with the fowls of heaven; yea, the fishes of the sea also shall be taken away. [4] Yet let no man strive, nor reprove another: for thy people are as they that strive with the priest. [5] Therefore shalt thou fall in the day, and the prophet also shall fall with thee in the night, and I will destroy thy mother. [6] My people are destroyed for lack of knowledge: because thou hast rejected knowledge, I will also reject thee, that thou shalt be no priest to me: seeing thou hast forgotten the law of thy God, I will also forget thy children.

The plan for success was simple.

Stay in his Word. Meditate in the Law, the word of God day and night. I love the word of God. I wish that I could spend time with each family sharing the word. It would be wonderful but it is not practical. We have Sunday school, home bible study and Wednesday night worship. I am teaching right now. I thank God for Teach The Word radio ministry. Often, I receive calls or meet people who listen to the broadcast every morning at 4:30 a.m. which is encouraging. Stay in his will. Live your life God's way, Jesus said.

John 14:6
Jesus saith unto him, I am the way, the truth, and the life: no man cometh unto the Father, but by me. God promises to stay with us. He is Emmanuel, God with us.

THE PROMISE

I will be with you wherever you go.

Joshua 1:3 again.
Every place that the sole of your foot shall tread upon, that have I given unto you, as I said unto Moses.

God told Joshua that every where his foot lands will be their possession! Would you say to Joshua "be careful do not go too far and take on too much". You would say to Joshua—"Go for the gold!"

Joshua 1:16-18
And they answered Joshua, saying, All that thou commandest us we will do, and whithersoever thou sendest us, we will go. [17] According as we hear-kened unto Moses in all things, so will we hearken unto thee: only the Lord thy God be with thee, as he was with Moses. [18] Whosoever he be that doth rebel against thy commandment, and will not hearken unto thy words in all that thou commandest him, he shall be put to death: only be strong and of a good courage. Every member should have this spirit, pastor, go for it and we are with you.

Did God keep his word to Joshua? Of course he did.

- He parted the Jordan river just like he did the Red Sea
- God gave them the city of Jericho by just marching
- God gave them victory over every enemy
- God gave each tribe their promised possession

Joshua's name means Jehovah saves. The Greek transliteration is Jesus!

Mark 6:31-42
And he said unto them, Come ye yourselves apart into a desert place, and rest a while: for there were many coming and going, and they had no leisure so much as to eat. [32] And they departed into a desert place by ship privately. [33] And the people saw them departing, and many knew him, and ran afoot thither out of all cities, and out went them, and came together unto him. [34] And Jesus, when he came out, saw much people, and was moved with com-passion toward them, because they were as sheep not having a shepherd: and

he began to teach them many things. [35] And when the day was now far spent, his disciples came unto him, and said, This is a desert place, and now the time is far passed: [36] Send them away, that they may go into the country round about, and into the villages, and buy themselves bread: for they have nothing to eat. [37] He answered and said unto them, Give ye them to eat. And they say unto him, Shall we go and buy two hundred pennyworth of bread, and give them to eat? [38] He saith unto them, How many loaves have ye? go and see. And when they knew, they said, Five, and two fishes. [39] And he commanded them to make all sit down by companies upon the green grass. [40] And they sat down in ranks, by hundreds, and by fifties. [41] And when he had taken the five loaves and the two fishes, he looked up to heaven, and blessed, and brake the loaves, and gave them to his disciples to set before them; and the two fishes divided he among them all. [42] And they did all eat, and were filled.

Jesus still saves. Jesus still provides. Jesus still blesses. He came to bless. He lived to bless. He died to bless. He rose to bless. He is coming back to bless. In the meantime, let us seek to bless. Brothers and sisters we have an opportunity to change the face of how church is done. It is not for our prestige but to change lives and give God glory. I promise you that if you follow my leadership then the blessings of God will be on all of our lives. Will you stand if you will support The Congregation Driven Ministry vision?

Part 4

The Tribal Concept for Today's Church

Numbers 13:1-16, 26-33

1. We cannot improve on God:

    a. his plan
    b. his promise
    c. his provision

2. Investigate the land:

    a. place
    b. people
    c. possibilities

3. The report:

    a. majority report

1. Fortified cities

2. Fear of giants

    b. minority report

1. Fruit

2. Faith

Conclusion: It is the church.

God! Just saying the word is powerful. God! God is! God is real! God is good! God is powerful! God is awesome! God is all-knowing! God is everywhere at the same time! God is a person! God speaks!

The fact that God communicates to his people is breathtaking. He reveals to his people, his plans, promises, purposes and provision. God! You cannot improve on God. There is no amount of fame or fortune that can take the place of God. You cannot improve on God. Everyday our society comes out with some product that is new and improved. You cannot improve on God. God gave his people a system that would ensure that all members of the congregation are covered by covenant. Even though the nation is several million strong, in God's eyes they are one congregation. (Numbers 13:26-27). In our text, God tells Moses that he is giving his people a land of promise. A land flowing with milk and honey. It is the Scripture's way of saying "A prime piece of real estate." God is establishing a people called by his name and a place. God tells Moses that he is giving them the land. God allows them to go and check out the land. They could have said, "Lord if you say it is flowing with milk and honey there is no need to check it out. Your word is good with us. We know that we cannot improve on you God." God will give us his plan so we can conclude for ourselves whether we are walking by faith not by sight.

THE PLAN

Moses selected a ruler from each tribe to investigate the land. They were men with leadership ability and courage. They were not the head of twelve cliques. There was no division among the group as it relates to their tribe. They were all for one and one for all. There were twelve tribes and a leader over each tribe. Moses was the leader over them all and God was over Moses! There was a clear line of authority and communication.

The plan was to send twelve men of good report to investigate the gift that God has promised them. When God gives you land, his promise is good. They could have taken out a line of credit on their land before they even saw it because God's promises are true.

THE PROMISE

I will evict the current occupants and give you title deed to the property. You just go check it out and see if it flows with milk and honey just as I said. The promises of God are true because they are based on his word. God cannot lie.

Heaven and earth would pass away before one word out of the mouth of God will fail. Is it not amazing that we will believe anybody but God.

THE PROVISION

God sends twelve tribe leaders to explore the land. They have no clue where they are going. They have never seen nor set foot on the land before but God miraculously leads them to where they need to go. They are spying the land for forty days and they have food, water and protection every day. All day and all night, the angels watch over them.

> Be not dismayed whatever betide
> God will take care of you
> Beneath his wings of love abide
> He will take care of you

Psalm 91:1-11
He that dwelleth in the secret place of the most High shall abide under the shadow of the Almighty. [2] I will say of the Lord, He is my refuge and my fortress: my God; in him will I trust. [3] Surely he shall deliver thee from the snare of the fowler, and from the noisome pestilence. [4] He shall cover thee with his feathers, and under his wings shalt thou trust: his truth shall be thy shield and buckler. [5] Thou shalt not be afraid for the terror by night; nor for the arrow that flieth by day; [6] Nor for the pestilence that walketh in darkness; nor for the destruction that wasteth at noonday. [7] A thousand shall fall at thy side, and ten thousand at thy right hand; but it shall not come nigh thee. [8] Only with thine eyes shalt thou behold and see the reward of the wicked. [9] Because thou hast made the Lord, which is my refuge, even the most High, thy habitation; [10] There shall no evil befall thee, neither shall any plague come nigh thy dwelling. [11] For he shall give his angels charge over thee, to keep thee in all thy ways.

INVESTIGATE THE LAND

Moses sends them to their promised land and instructs them to check it out and see if God can be trusted. Determine if God is telling you the truth. Prove God and take him at his word. First, look at the land and see if it is good. Look at the people and see if God can evict them. Look at the land and see the possibilities.

EDEN REVISITED

Genesis 2:15-17
And the Lord God took the man, and put him into the garden of Eden to dress it and to keep it. [16] And the Lord God commanded the man, saying, Of every tree of the garden thou mayest freely eat: [17] But of the tree of the knowledge of good and evil, thou shalt not eat of it: for in the day that thou eatest thereof thou shalt surely die.

God is giving them another garden. One hundred fifty miles long and sixty miles wide. The possibilities are mind-blowing. They will live in houses that they did not build. Eat crops that they did not plant. Drink from wells that will never run dry—a land flowing with milk and honey. The tribe concept is God's plan to care for each member of the congregation with no one left behind. It will not form cliques as long as leaders follow God and leadership.

THE REPORT

They came back with fruit so large that it took two men to carry it between two poles. Listen to their report, "We found the land and it does flow with milk and honey just as God said. Here is some of the fruit of the land that God gave us. Nevertheless ... the people are strong (doubt) the cities are walled (dismay) and giants are in the land (defeat) tribe members we cannot possess the land(discouragement)."

Note that they have not fought a battle and have had no personal contact with the inhabitants of the land. Yet, we hear doubt, dismay, defeat and discouragement.

Unbelief sees only obstacles but faith sees opportunities. (Warren Wiersbe).

Ten of the twelve-tribe leaders brought back the fruit of the land but also the fruit of fear. However, Joshua and Caleb brought back the fruit of faith.

Numbers 13:30
And Caleb stilled the people before Moses, and said, Let us go up at once, and possess it; for we are well able to overcome it.

When doubt is given a hearing it breeds fear. The plan, promise and purposes of God has no influence among God's people. Fear is a cancer that will eat up faith and leave only unbelief. If only they had known.

Psalm 121:1-8

A Song of Degrees

I will lift up mine eyes unto the hills, from whence cometh my help. [2] My help cometh from the Lord, which made heaven and earth. [3] He will not suffer thy foot to be moved: he that keepeth thee will not slumber. [4] Behold, he that keepeth Israel shall neither slumber nor sleep. [5] The Lord is thy keeper: the Lord is thy shade upon thy right hand. [6] The sun shall not smite thee by day, nor the moon by night. [7] The Lord shall preserve thee from all evil: he shall preserve thy soul. [8] The Lord shall preserve thy going out and thy coming in from this time forth, and even for evermore.

Conclusion

All God was trying to do was bless his people. He gave them a leader in Moses and leaders of each tribe. He said that they were his people and the sheep of his pasture. He was giving them a place to call home. They spied the land for forty days and brought back unbelief. God told them that since you did not believe me, I will cause you to wander one year for each day. So they wandered in the wilderness for forty years. They traveled in an eleven-mile circle for forty years! All God was doing was trying to make the congregation a church. A place to belong. A place to find community. A place to find love and acceptance. A place to train their children. A place to grow. A place to worship. A place to pray. A place to fellowship.

Matthew 16:18

And I say also unto thee, that thou art Peter, and upon this rock I will build my church; and the gates of hell shall not prevail against it.

I thank God for the church. Jesus founded the church. He is the head of the church. He gave his life for the church. He died on the cross for the church. He rose for the church. He is coming back for the church. You must be in Christ and in the church. The tribes can help us be the church. Get in one and let God bless you.

Transitions

Leading your Church through Change

Step 1: Preparing for Change

- Condition of your Church
- Concerns of your membership
- Commitment of your laity
- Call to biblical discipleship
- Commitment to honor God

Key: Prepare but don't rush!

Step 2: Define Your Vision (one sentence)

- Discover your purpose ... what to do?
- Define your "target" group ... who will do?
- Decide your strategy ... how to do?

Key: To be dynamic you must be specific.

Step 3: Plant the Vision

- Secure the support you need
- Secure the assistance you need
- Secure the advice you need

Key: Expose your leaders to other models.

Step 4: Share the Vision

- Core leaders
- Extended leaders
- Whole Church

Key: Use multiple mediums to share the vision.

Step 5: Start the Process of Change

- Make one major change at a time
- Make sure people are in the right place
- Use the 5 R's

Key: Build on your strengths.

Step 6: Expect Opposition

- Experience: apathy, anger, criticism, attacks, fights
- Respond: prayer, patience, encouragement, perseverance

Key: Remind people why you are making changes. Celebrate success!

Motivation for Ministry

1 Corinthians 15:51-58

Some subjects we do not like to discuss. We avoid this subject like a plague. You will not find it in the curriculum of pre-school, kindergarten, junior or high school. The subject that we do not like to discuss is the one thing that none of us can avoid. Yes, I am talking about death. We never think that children are ready to talk about it. The young people think it will never happen to them. Older people think you are trying to get rid of them if you ask them about death. Talking about death makes us all uncomfortable. We must talk about it. The bible teaches that it is appointed for all men to die and then be judged.

Three usual responses:

- You will live forever!
- I do not want to talk about it!
- What will I get when you are gone?

The believer should be able to talk comfortably about death because Jesus came to earth to die. The one time we want to discuss death is when we are least ready to do it. When our world is falling apart, we say, "I wish I was dead". However, when life is good, we do not want to hear about death and dying. When someone dies, we say he or she passed away. The physicians use the term, expired. We hide cemeteries on distant hills, behind high walls, on the outskirts of town so as not to think about the "D" word. The Christian faith is "R" rated.

- We are rejoicing people.
- We are recovering people.
- We are rejuvenating people.
- We are repaying people.
- We are resurrection people.

Death is a real enemy, but when Jesus rose on Sunday morning he defeated death. Dr. Martin Luther King, Jr. stated, that if we have not found a cause that we are willing to die for, then we are not ready to live.

Paul writes to this church in Corinth, because someone was teaching that the resurrection was past. Others were teaching that it never happened. The believers were told that all of those who died in Christ were lost because once you are dead you are done. The result was that the church had become stagnant. Some stopped working. Many others started sinning willfully. They lost their motivation for ministry. What we believe, affects our behavior. Our doctrine determines our duty. Paul writes:

1 Corinthians 15:16-19
For if the dead rise not, then is not Christ raised: [17] And if Christ be not raised, your faith is vain; ye are yet in your sins. [18] Then they also which are fallen asleep in Christ are perished. [19] If in this life only we have hope in Christ, we are of all men most miserable.

The Apostle is teaching that until we handle our death and resurrection business we will not be motivated for ministry.

The Transformation

Listen, I will show you a mystery: we will not all sleep or die but we will all be changed. Death is not the end for the child of God. Quick, faster than fast, in the blink of your eyelid you will be changed. Job believed this:

Job 14:10-15
But man dieth, and wasteth away: yea, man giveth up the ghost, and where is he? [11] As the waters fail from the sea, and the flood decayeth and drieth up: [12] So man lieth down, and riseth not: till the heavens be no more, they shall not awake, nor be raised out of their sleep. [13] Oh that thou wouldest hide me in the grave, that thou wouldest keep me secret, until thy wrath be past, that thou wouldest appoint me a set time, and remember me! [14] If a man die, shall he live again? all the days of my appointed time will I wait, till my change come. [15] Thou shalt call, and I will answer thee: thou wilt have a desire to the work of thine hands.

Flesh and blood cannot inherit the kingdom of God. As the line in the movie goes—Everyone wants to go to heaven but we do not want to go dead.

- Flesh must give way to spirit.
- Mortal must give way to immortality.
- Corruption must give way to incorruption.
- Life gives way to death.

- Death gives way to resurrection.

The good news of the gospel is your best is yet to come. No matter how well you have it on earth, this is not as good as it gets.

Our transformation is to start now. Since you have been born again, you are to live like it.

- Consecrate each day that God allows you to wake up. Do not believe Satan's lie that you are too busy to start your day with God. If you give God the impression that you are too busy for him, when you need him he may tell you that he is too busy for you.
- Commit the day to the Lord.

Psalm 37:5-6
Commit thy way unto the Lord; trust also in him; and he shall bring it to pass. [6] And he shall bring forth thy righteousness as the light, and thy judgment as the noonday.

Tell the Lord that you need him every hour. Tell him that you love him. Tell him that with out him you will fail.

- Communicate your love of the Lord to other people. Without being over religious, ask God for opportunities to share your love of him with friends and family. Testify of his goodness to you.

THANKSGIVING

Listen to the joyous ring of thanksgiving. Paul is shouting right here. He uses the word victory three times.

Death is swallowed up in victory. O grave where is your victory. Thanks be to God who gives us the victory!

You cannot talk about victory without a shout. Our faith is no cold, formal, legal transaction. It is a heart changing, blood rushing, mind-blowing experience. I dare you to let Jesus into your heart and give him full control.

V.I.C.T.O.R.Y.

V. VISION—look at life from God's view

I. INFLUENCE—character of Christ

C. COMMITMENT—to live for God's glory and not earthly pleasure

T. TIME—use your time wisely

O. OPPORTUNITY—take advantage of doors that God opens

R. RESOURCES—use everything you have to advance God's kingdom

Y. YOU—you are ALL you have. Kirk Nowery

When you think about the goodness of God it will lead you to thank God. When you t-h-i-n-k, you will t-h-a-n-k.

The victory is ours through Jesus Christ. Jesus has done the hard part:

- He was born of a virgin … that was hard.
- He taught in the temple at twelve … that was hard.
- He turned water into wine … that was hard.
- He fed five thousand with two fish and five biscuits … that was hard.
- He cured blindness … that was hard.
- He suffered under Pilate … that was hard.
- He went to Calvary … that was hard.
- He died … that was hard.
- He rose … that was hard.

THE TRIUMPH

Therefore, based on these facts, here is the only logical response. Death is defeated. Soul is saved. Victory is secure. Heaven is yours. Therefore, since your sins are all forgiven, no condemnation, you must say yes to God's word, will and way.

- Be steadfast.
- Be immovable.
- Always abounding, in the Lord's work.
- Labor in the Lord is not in vain.

Paul shouts:

Philippians 3:10

That I may know him, and the power of his resurrection, and the fellowship of his sufferings, being made conformable unto his death;

- We know! We are in the "we know" crowd!
- We know that God is good (Ps.100:5)
- We know that the trying of our faith works patience (James 1:3)
- We know that he will not put more on us than we can bear (1 Cor. 10:13)
- We know that he knows the way we take (Job 23:10)
- We know that weeping may endure for a night but we know joy comes in the morning light (Proverbs 30:5)
- And we know that all things work together for good to them that love God, to them who are the called according to his purpose. (Romans 8:28)
- We know tribulation works patience, not our nerves!
- We know that when this life is over, we have a building not made with hands, eternal in the heavens.
- We know of a place where hearst wheels never roll, cancer cells cannot grow, and it is a land where we never grow old.

"I hear what you are saying pastor, but I am going through it right now. I am tired and I want to give up. I hear you say that I ought to be motivated for ministry. God has been good to me, but I am tired. I am weary. I want to throw in the towel." Do not give in, give up or give out. One grandmother told her grandchild that was about to stop serving the Lord because of hardships— "When you feel like giving up go the Shall station." He said. "Granny, I do not need gas I need strength." She said, "Son go to the Shall station."

- The Lord is my shepherd, I shall not want
- For in the time of trouble, He shall hide me
- The Lord is my light and my salvation, whom shall I fear
- Purge me with hyssop, and I shall be clean, wash me, and I shall be whiter than snow
- The just shall live by faith

Isaiah 40:28-31
Hast thou not known? hast thou not heard, that the everlasting God, the Lord, the Creator of the ends of the earth, fainteth not, neither is weary? there is no searching of his understanding. [29] He giveth power to the faint; and to them that have no might he increaseth strength. [30] Even the youths shall faint and be weary, and the young men shall utterly fall: [31] But they that wait upon the Lord shall renew their strength; they shall mount up with wings as eagles; they shall run, and not be weary; and they shall walk, and not faint.

Pull into the "shall" station and fill up:

- Love
- Joy
- Peace
- Patience
- Gentleness
- Goodness
- Faith
- Meekness
- Self-control

Fill up! Fill up! Fill up and go to work for the Lord!

Recovering Lost Power

Text: Matthew 17:14-21

1. The Case:

    a. petition for mercy
    b. presence of misery
    c. powerless ministry

2. The Cause:

    a. authority of call
    b. anointing is missing
    c. absence of intimacy

3. The Cure:

    a. return to the mission
    b. remove any hindrance (lay aside weight)
    c. rediscover his power

Conclusion: Faith, living, growing, believing.

Sickness makes me sick. Whenever I visit a home or a hospital and a beloved person is stricken with illness it makes me sick. Often I have prayed for people and they have recovered but not always. I know that death is a reality but sickness still makes me sick. I am studying the gospels again. I am in Matthew's gospel presently. I am struck with the frequency of Jesus' healing.

- Matthew 4:23-24
- And Jesus went about all Galilee, teaching in their synagogues, and preaching the gospel of the kingdom, and healing all manner of sickness and all manner of disease among the people. [24] And his fame

went throughout all Syria: and they brought unto him all sick people that were taken with divers diseases and torments, and those which were possessed with devils, and those which were lunatic, and those that had the palsy; and he healed them.

(All passages in the gospel of Matthew)
- 8:1-2 He cleansed a leper.
- 8:7 Centurion's servant.
- 8:15 Peter's mother-in-law.
- 8:16 He healed many.
- 8:32 Two demon possessed men.
  9:2, 9:22, 9:29, 9:33

- 9 Paralyzed man, a woman with a bleeding problem, two blind men, and a possessed man.
- 12:13 A man with a withered hand, the list goes on and on.

In chapter ten he gave the twelve disciples power over sickness, demons, and disease.

I wrestled with the Lord and this text. Lord, we have more disease, demons and death today than ever before. The text that I am teaching was my answer. We have lost our God given power. God still loves and cares for his own. Great gifts come with the price tag of great responsibility.

THE CASE

Jesus took Peter, James and John up to a high mountain and left the other nine behind. I do not know how the other disciples felt about not being invited up but we can imagine. He was transfigured before them. He showed the three his glory—his heaven side. Moses and Elijah appeared with Jesus and Peter wanted to build three permanent memorials on the site. But Moses and Elijah vanished and Jesus stood alone. A voice out of the cloud said, "This is my beloved son hear him!" After coming down the mountain, they see a large crowd. Out of that crowd came a man running up to Jesus and he kneeled down in a worshipful position. He asked for mercy, not for himself but for his son. When we need mercy, the Lord Jesus is the source we should seek. Listen to the Psalmist:

Psalm 86:3-5
Be merciful unto me, O Lord: for I cry unto thee daily. [4] Rejoice the soul of thy servant: for unto thee, O Lord, do I lift up my soul. [5] For thou, Lord, art good, and ready to forgive; and plenteous in mercy unto all them that call upon thee.

Psalm 86:15
But thou, O Lord, art a God full of compassion, and gracious, longsuffering, and plenteous in mercy and truth.

The story of the demon- possessed boy is located in Matthew, Mark and Luke. We know that he is an only son. He is called an epileptic. He suffers from a spiritual malady that is attributed to demons. He is suicidal when under their influence. When he is close to water, he jumps in. When he gets near fire, he will fall in. "I brought him to your disciples but they could not cure him." Now remember that Jesus had given them power over spirits. He sent them out to cure diseases and he was not with them. Jesus did not need to be present for them to be powerful! They tried to cast out the demon, but the condition did not improve. A crowd is now gathered. The more they tried, the more frustrated they became. The Pharisees arrived on the scene to make a bad situation worse. "What? You are his disciples and you can not help anyone?"

JESUS' RESPONSE

Faithless and crooked generation, how long must I put up with this? Jesus expected them to be able to heal the boy! Could it be that he expects us to be able to do something about the ills of our day? Some believe that God can heal but he is no longer in the healing business. He has turned it over to the medical community. Some believe that he still heals, but you never know whom he might heal so you pray and hope for the best. Some claim the gift of healing, but they have to take up a large offering in a large stadium to cover expenses. Doctor's as well as the evangelist have to have an offering before they try. Since God did give his disciples healing power, what has happened? There is no evidence in scripture that says that healing is over. In fact, the opposite is true!

John 14:12-16
Verily, verily, I say unto you, He that believeth on me, the works that I do shall he do also; and greater works than these shall he do; because I go unto my Father. [13] And whatsoever ye shall ask in my name, that will I do, that the Father may be glorified in the Son. [14] If ye shall ask any thing in my name, I

will do it. [15] If ye love me, keep my commandments. [16] And I will pray the Father, and he shall give you another Comforter, that he may abide with you forever.

The Cause

Jesus said, "Bring him to me!" When there is a serious accident, the EMT is called. When there is a four-alarm fire, the fire department is called. When there is criminal activity, the police are called. When there is a spiritual emergency, Jesus must be called!

Bring him to me. Bring it to me. Bring them to me. Bring all to me. Even if the church fails, if the members fail, if the preacher fails, there is no failure in God.

Why could the disciples not heal the man? They asked the Lord themselves, why could we not cast it out?

They had the authority of a call. They were selected after an all night prayer meeting. They received on the job training from the master. They had prior success. What happened? Well, they had authority, but the anointing was missing. While the Lord was away, they ceased their prayer communion. While the Lord was away, they stopped worshipping. While the Lord was away, they discontinued their study habits. While the Lord was away, they became self-reliant. They became disconnected by becoming involved in the cares of the world. May I ask you, "What are you doing for the Lord while he is away?" Their faith became inactive and then non-existent.

Hebrews 11:6
But without faith it is impossible to please him: for he that cometh to God must believe that he is, and that he is a rewarder of them that diligently seek him.

I want to commend the nine. They may have gotten out of fellowship, but they were concerned enough to want to know why they could not do their job.

We need to be reminded that prayerlessness leads to powerlessness.

People need the church. People need spirit-filled people around them. The diseased person needs you. The demon-possessed person needs you. The discouraged person needs you. The dependent personality needs you. The Lord needs you.

THE CURE

Rev. 2:1-4

Unto the angel of the church of Ephesus write: These things saith he that holdeth the seven stars in his right hand, who walketh in the midst of the seven golden candlesticks; [2] I know thy works, and thy labour, and thy patience, and how thou canst not bear them which are evil: and thou hast tried them which say they are apostles, and are not, and hast found them liars: [3] And hast borne, and hast patience, and for my name's sake hast laboured, and hast not fainted. [4] Nevertheless I have somewhat against thee, because thou hast left thy first love.

We must return to the mission of Christ. We have allowed the pursuit of fame, fashion, finance and fun to rob us of both gift and grace. We must lay aside every weight and the sin that so easily beset us, and run this race with patience looking unto Jesus the author and finisher of our faith.

Jesus told them that this kind comes not out except by prayer and fasting. It will come out but not without personal discipline. The good news is that it will come out.

- That habit will come out.
- That attitude will come out.
- That craving will come out.
- That sickness will come out.
- That demonic bondage will come out.

Satan's lie is that your struggle today will be your struggle forever.

We must make prayer the most important work of the church. After we get off our knees, we must go out and make a difference. Who knows what gift God may give us to do his will. There are hundreds of prayers in the bible, but they will not help us if we do not pray. Jesus came to teach us to pray.

Matthew 6:9-13
After this manner therefore pray ye: Our Father which art in heaven, Hallowed be thy name. [10] Thy kingdom come. Thy will be done in earth, as it is in heaven. [11] Give us this day our daily bread. [12] And forgive us our debts, as we forgive our debtors. [13] And lead us not into temptation, but deliver us from evil: For thine is the kingdom, and the power, and the glory, forever. Amen.

Jesus died so that we could pray. He is at the right hand of the father waiting for us to pray. A preacher friend told the story of how we can learn to pray from a bird. A bird can be up a tree, out on a limb, in heavy rain, with fierce wind, in the dark, and never fall out of the tree. How? The bird has talons that are claw like. He grips the branch and then he bends his knees. The winds may blow, the rain may fall, it may get darker than a thousand midnights but if you hold on and bend your knees, you can make it.

> Come on church, let us bend our knees.
> Come what will or may bend your knees.
> Are you lost ... bend
> Are you weak ... bend
> Are you lonely ... bend
> Need a blessing ... bend
> Just bend your knees

Text: John 18:37
Title: A Date with Destiny

1. Person with a purpose:

    a. Discover it

    b. Disrupt it

    c. Disaster without it

2. Purpose does not prohibit problems:

    a. Confusion

    b. Challenge

    c. Change

3. Power to fulfill purpose:

    a. Within

    b. Withstand

    c. Witness

Conclusion: Keep the Date!

We have just celebrated the birth of Jesus. Our Christmas worship was an awe-some experience. I am thankful that we celebrated him on the day we set aside for him. I believe that our hearts are right with God, therefore, we are blessed. There are two passages that have come together for me as never before. I want to share a message that can change someone's destiny.

Matthew 2:1-2
Now when Jesus was born in Bethlehem of Judaea in the days of Herod the King, behold, there came wise men from the east to Jerusalem [2] saying, Where is he that is born King of the Jews? For we have seen his star in the east, and are come to worship him.

John 18:37
Pilate therefore said unto him, Art thou a king then? Jesus answered, Thou sayest that I am a king. To this end was I born, and for this cause came I into the world, that I should bear witness unto the truth. Everyone that is of the truth heareth my voice.

Our parents tell us our birth date. We do not know our death date. There is a date that is more important than either date. That is our date with destiny. Each person is born with a date with destiny. It is the most important of the three dates, because if we do not discover our destiny, then life will have little or no meaning. When we discover our destiny life has purpose. Rick Warren's book, The Purpose Driven Life touches a nerve because most people will live and die without ever knowing the purpose for their birth. Pontius Pilate asked Jesus a question that holds life-changing meaning. Are you really a king? The wise men said he was born a king. Pilate is asking, did you make it? Did you reach your destiny? Jesus said, I AM, I AM a King. He gives two truths in one sentence. I AM, I AM a King. Jesus made it. He became what God intended for him. He came to earth for a purpose and he fulfilled it. When we discover our purpose, our life has meaning and focus. There is a growing problem among our youth. Many of them are taking their lives, because the life that they are living has little or no meaning. When we refuse to give God, control of our lives, we disrupt the purpose that he intended for us from the foundation of the world. Our birth is neither an accident nor a mistake. God knew us from eternity. Our life is just a disaster waiting to happen when we refuse God's plan and purpose for our lives. Fame, fortune or family cannot replace pur-pose. Education, entertainment or easy living will not replace purpose. Jesus tells Pilate, I was born to be a king and that is who I am. Parents have the responsibility to help each child discover their reason for existence. It is not enough to clothe, feed, shelter, educate and entertain them. Parents can enable their children to discover their purpose if the parent is living a life of purpose. Modeling is key to success. Parents, what does your child learn about life by looking at your life?

In this scripture, Jesus states his purpose but he is standing before a court of death. When you discover your purpose in life, it does not mean that your problems are over. Often, you have to go through problems to get to your purpose.

Jesus is teaching and they interrupt him:

Mark 3:31-35
There came then his brethren and his mother and, standing without, sent unto him, calling him. [32] And the multitude sat about him, and they said unto him, Behold, thy mother and thy brethren without seek for thee. [33] And he answered them, saying, Who is my mother or my brethren? [34] And he looked round about on them which sat about him, and said, Behold my mother and my brethren! [35] For whosoever shall do the will of God, the same is my brother, and my sister, and my mother.

1. Sometimes you have to redefine your family to fulfill your purpose.

His protégé Peter told him that he did not have to die. Jesus told Peter to get behind him.

2. Sometimes you have to change friends to fulfill your purpose.

The Scribes and the Pharisees wanted to hold onto useless traditions. Jesus said, you have heard that you should love your friends and hate your enemies. I say, love your enemies, pray for them, feed them, even clothe them.

3. Sometimes you have to change things to fulfill your destiny.

- Jesus is standing before Pilate facing condemnation
- Before that, his followers deserted him
- Before that, they went to sleep on him
- Before that, they wanted a free lunch
- Before that, all they wanted was healing.

- Before that, he was called a drunk.
- Before that, he was called a devil.

Jesus still met his date with destiny! For this reason was I born! Jesus says to Pilate, I AM. Remember that is the name that the Lord gave Moses when he asked. "Whom should I say is sending me to Pharaoh?" The Lord said, "Tell him that I AM sent you."

Jesus is telling Pilate, "The same I AM that sent Moses is standing before you right now."

- I AM the son of God.
- I AM the bread of life.
- I AM the light of the world.
- I AM water in dry places.
- I AM the lily of the valley.
- I AM the bright and morning star.
- I just AM.

Jesus gives us the keys to knowing and fulfilling our destiny. The power is within.

ILLUSTRATION

The famous sculptor Michelangelo was standing before a huge marble stone without shape. Someone asked what he expected to get out of it. Michelangelo said that there is an angel inside of the marble and it was his task to get it out. Sitting in this room today are people whom God has ordained a date with destiny and you just have to let him bring it out!

Do not settle for less than your divine purpose.

- In spite of what you have gone through, you have a date
- In spite of your past problems or your present predicament, you still have a date
- In spite of your parents, your age, your gender, your race, your education or lack of it, you still have a date. Your marital status does not limit you from keeping the date.

Jesus told Pilate that he was in control. I was born for this reason, to bear witness to the truth. And those who want to know the truth will listen to me.

- I have a date with you Pilate, but one day you will have a date with me, You are judging me today, but one day I will judge you.
- I have a date with a cross.
- I have a date with a tomb.
- I have a resurrection date.

You and I have a birth date, a death date and a destiny date. The first two you can not do anything about. But the destiny date is in your hands! Keep that date!

Conclusion

It is both my observation and experience that Seminary does not prepare pastors to develop healthy churches. It is due, in part, to the fact that Christian educators are more familiar with theory than the practice of ministry. Many churches perish for lack of a ministry plan. Dr. A.L. Patterson has said, that we are born originals but die carbon copies. The reality is that ministers attempt to grow their churches through "techniques" they learn at church growth conferences. We learn from one another. This is a wise and biblical practice. However, what works in one church may not help another one, especially if the methods are put together in a "Frankenstein" sort of way. When Jesus affirmed that he would build his church, he had a method in mind. He taught that a proper foundation must be laid. Paul later echoed this sentiment in warning the Corinthians to be careful how they built their church.

1 Cor. 3:9-14
For we are labourers together with God: ye are God's husbandry, ye are God's building. [10] According to the grace of God which is given unto me, as a wise master builder, I have laid the foundation, and another buildeth thereon. But let every man take heed how he buildeth thereupon. [11] For other foundation can no man lay than that is laid, which is Jesus Christ. [12] Now, if any man build upon this foundation gold, silver, precious stones, wood, hay stubble; [13] Every man's work shall be made manifest: for the day shall declare it, because it shall be revealed by fire; and the fire shall try every man's work of what sort it is. [14] If any man's work abide which he hath built thereupon, he shall receive a reward.

In The Congregation Driven Ministry, a plan to start, to grow and evaluate ministry is put forth. The methods are biblical and proven. They have been presented across nondenominational and nonracial lines. The church's landscape is confusing at this time in history. The path to God is not clear. The Kingdom of God is near, yet so far away. We must preach Christ and him crucified. We must not abandon the cross to remain in step with an inoffensive religious culture. We must return to the biblical admonition to place ministry in the hands of the people. Ministry should be done for the people by the people. The pastor is a gift from God, but he/she is not the Commander-in-Chief of the Lord's army. The pastor must pray, plan and proclaim according to Acts 6. It is then, and only then, that he/she can be an effective weapon in spiritual warfare. It is my hope that this work will continue a much-needed discussion on how to do "church" in this period in history. There are many options open to us. We can choose to do nothing, We can become his peculiar people and a chosen generation. (1 Peter 2:9) In the final analysis, we the people of God, must take responsibility for the church's mission and become accountable to each other. The people of God under the anointing of the Holy Spirit can rise up and become an exceedingly great army. (Ezekiel 37:10)

Bibliography

Burke, Dale H. Less Is More Leadership. Eugene, Oregon: Harvest House Publishers, 2004.

Derickson, Gary, and Radmacher, Earl. The Disciplemaker: What Matters Most to Jesus. Salem, Oregon: Charis Press, 2001.

Finzel, Hans. The Top Ten Mistakes Leaders Make. Wheaton, Illinois: Victor Books, 1994.

Frye, J.W. Jesus the Pastor: Leading Others in the Character & Power of Christ. Grand Rapids, Michigan: Zondervan Publishing House, 2000.

London, Jr., H.B., Wiseman, Neil B. The Heart of a Great Pastor: How to Grow Strong and Thrive Wherever God Has Planted You. Ventura, California: Regal Books, 1994.

Manning, Brennan. Ruthless Trust: The Ragamuffin's Path to God. New York, New York: Harper Collins Publishers, Inc., 2000.

McCalep, Jr., Ph.D., George O. Church Growth Made Simple: Twenty Simple Changes Guaranteed to Transform Your Church. Lithonia, Georgia: Orman Press, 2005.

Miller, Calvin. The Empowered Leader: 10 Keys to Servant Leadership. Nashville, Tennessee: Broadman & Holman Publishers, 1995.

Pope, Randy. The Prevailing Church: An Alternative Approach to Ministry. Chicago, Illinois: Moody Press, 2002.

Wagner, Peter C. Your Spiritual Gifts Can Help Your Church Grow. Ventura, California: Regal Books, 1979.

Warren, Rick. The Purpose Driven Church: Growth without Compromising Your Message & Mission. Grand Rapids, Michigan: Zondervan Publishing House, 1995.

Warren, Rick. The Purpose Driven Life: What on Earth Am I Here For? Grand Rapids, Michigan: Zondervan Publishing House, 2002.

Appendix

Pilgrim Baptist Church

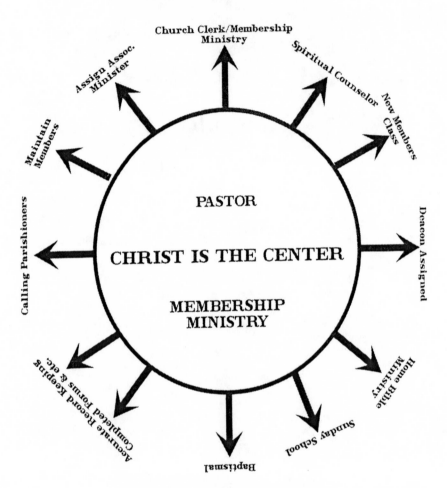

Church Clerk/Membership Ministry

Assign Assoc. Minister

Spiritual Counselor

New Members Class

Maintain Members

Calling Parishioners

PASTOR

CHRIST IS THE CENTER

MEMBERSHIP MINISTRY

Deacon Assigned

Accurate Record Keeping Completed forms & etc.

Home Bible Ministry

Baptismal

Sunday School

Rev. Dr. Larry W. Ellis, Pastor

Pilgrim Baptist Church

Reverend Dr. Larry Wayne Ellis, Senior Pastor

2006 ANNUAL REPORT

TABLE OF CONTENTS

Message from Dr. Larry W. Ellis, Pastor

I hardly have the words to express just how much I appreciate the collective work completed at Pilgrim in 2006. The Lord is blessing us. We have an excellent leadership team, a dedicated church staff, and a faithful church body. Great things happened last year. Trusting God for all things, the leadership team put together a God-size budget of one million dollars. How fitting that we reached that milestone during our 80th year of ministry! We have come a long way financially, haven't we? God continued to bless Pilgrim as we established our first endowed college scholarship fund. This fund will ensure that all our students who are ready and able to continue their education after graduating from high school will have funds to afford that.

What troubles my heart the most this year is that we are reaching only 60% of our potential. Thirty percent of the congregation comes to Sunday service or on special occasions but just leave. I am concerned not just for their inactivity but also for their salvation. We have to really work to get the inactive members involved. Can you imagine the possibilities if 250 more people attended Sunday School and Home Bible Study and were involved in one or two ministries? I welcome your thoughts on what we can do. Please pray with me for wisdom and guidance in this matter. God expects more of us than just coming to church, for faith without works is dead. James 2:23 illustrates James's faith and actions were working together, and his faith was made complete by what he did (James 2:24). You see, a person is justified by what he does and not by faith alone.

The Lord was truly gracious to me in 2006. He has allowed me to be at Pilgrim for 20 years. I was installed as president of the California Congress of Christian Education. In this role I want to take Christian education to a deeper level. I will share some of Pilgrim's best practices with other churches. Samford University selected me as a recipient of their National Pastoral Excellence Award and Sabbath Leave Program. This means that I will be away for the last three months of 2007. This time in Alabama will be devoted to study, writing and growing. This will also be time of reflection, refreshing and renewal.

I am excited about what the future holds. Pilgrim will continue to place emphasis on education, economic development (on the Pilgrim Organization, Inc. side) health and well being. We are going to be called upon by God to do things that other churches are unable to do. We have the potential to reach $2 million per year within five to six years. It is going to be a good ride – sometimes bumpy but still good. I believe that God will do it again.

Continue to care for your family and for one another. Everybody is important!

To God Be the Glory!

Love,

Pastor Ellis

2009 PILGRIM BAPTIST ANNUAL REPORT

80 Years of Obedient Service
1926 - 2007

On December 31, 1926, the late A. J. Lucas opened his 147 North Fremont Street home to neighbors for a simple spirited Watch Night Service. Mr. Lucas could not have known what a mighty work God had begun with this humble gesture. Mr. Lucas reached out and God responded. Four months later, the first Baptist church in San Mateo to be a focus for African-Americans was founded. From Reverend Dean, to each succeeding pastor, the church flourished. There were bumps in the road, but the Lord used them to strengthen the church.

Reverend Sample distinguished Pilgrim Baptist Church as a prime church. Each of the succeeding pastors left their mark on the church, some greater than others. After a yearlong and exhaustive search, in 1987 Pilgrim had a new pastor who was surely anointed by the Lord, Reverend Doctor Larry Wayne Ellis. He relinquished his ministry post at Mount Zion to come lead Pilgrim. God gave him visions of what the church could be. As a talented visionary, Pastor Ellis leads the way drawing people into a closer walk and deeper relationship with Jesus. He teaches the Word accurately and simply so worshipers can easily understand it. Pastor Ellis gives practical application on how to stay in God's will. He shows a path toward becoming a matured Christian.

Pastor Ellis saw that Pilgrim must take steps in response to our expanding numbers and diverse congregation. New members were at varying levels of faith and Bible knowledge. Hence, multiple avenues for spiritual development were adopted. Pastor Ellis introduced the "Congregation Driven Ministry" concept as the basis for member ministry participation and spiritual growth. He preached the value of being in church every Sunday. He required all leaders and encouraged others to attend Sunday School and join Home Bible Study. Another vision evidenced in 2000 was midweek service for those who are unable to attend on Sunday. Wednesday Night Service also attracts many of the Sunday worshipers. An added benefit is that Prayer Meeting before service has larger numbers now praying.

The 12 Tribe model launched last year (to ensure proper attention is paid to members and families), continues to evolve. Tribes lead part of Wednesday Night service. They gather on fifth Sundays during Sunday School hour. Deacons with Trustees as co-leaders, help Tribes mature and win over lost souls. Tribes also gather outside of church for fellowship, praise, prayer, and to provide support to members as needed.

Pastor Ellis imagined the weekly radio ministry expanding to daily broadcasts. Now, "Teach the Word" is heard Monday through Friday at 4:30 a.m. and Sunday at 5:30 p.m. on KFAX-1100AM. He is touching thousands beyond Pilgrim's walls.

Always looking ahead, Pastor Ellis requested that an exploratory committee study and recommend the ideal facility for Pilgrim's projected growth over the next three to five years. They will offer a plan in 2007 for a new church facility relative to size, location and factoring in membership demography.

April 4, 1926

Reverend Z. Dean, the first pastor, established the church and named it Abyssinia Missionary Baptist.

1926-1933

Reverend Dean was the second pastor, followed by Reverends Davis, McCall, Allen and Hubbard, who all uniquely influenced.

1933-1965

Reverend W. C. Sample renamed the church to Pilgrim Baptist Church. The current church building was constructed in 1962 and membership increased to 400.

1965-1975

Reverend Arthur L. Jarrell, Jr. continued to increase membership before leaving to form a new church.

1975-1986

Reverend John Cooper, Jr. encouraged leaders to become active in all church matters, paid off mortgage and bought other properties.

1986-1987

Reverend W. P. Cook was interim pastor. Church leaders formally prayed for the right pastor. Parsonage underwent $60,000 renovation.

September 4, 1987 - Present

Reverend Doctor Larry Wayne Ellis was a prayer answered. He has been teaching, preaching, leading and transforming Pilgrim into a Five-Star church in all his endeavors over the last 20 years.

5

Looking Ahead in 2007 and Beyond

Leadership Worth Following: *"We are Grateful for the Journey."* – Hebrews 13:7

Pilgrim Baptist Church will honor Pastor Ellis and First Lady Van in September for 20 years of anointed service. The celebration committee has many wonderful treats in store.

- The Music, Fine Arts and Media Ministry will offer up a musical extravaganza like none before.
- Plans are in the works for a great celebration banquet for July.
- Other activities are scheduled throughout the month of September culminating in the Pastor and Wife's 20th Anniversary service on September 23.

The committee wants Pastor Ellis and First Lady to have tangible proof of our love and appreciation for them both. Thus, each member is asked to give $10 for each year Pastor Ellis has shepherded Pilgrim, a total of $200. Individuals naturally must judge what he or she can afford. Give only what can be given cheerfully.

Pastor Awarded Coveted Fellowship

Pastor is a recipient of one of the most prestigious awards bestowed to a church pastor. The award requires excellence in preaching, teaching and leading – that has Pastor Ellis. He will go to Beeson Divinity School at Samford University, Birmingham, Alabama for three months this fall. The time will be devoted to studying, writing and reflecting. He, too, will be ministered to. While in Alabama during, Pastor Ellis and First Lady will have their first experience of sitting side-by-side for all those glorious consecutive Sundays worshiping like other married couples. When they return in January 2008, Pastor Ellis and First Lady will be reinvigorated and rejuvenated. Truly the church will be the benefactors of this prestigious award.

Money No Longer a College Barrier

Pastor Ellis was made aware that some of our college-bound and college students faced financial problems significant enough to keep them out of college. In Pastor's words, "Every child in Pilgrim who is capable and wants to go to college should have the chance to go." So he shared his idea of an endowed scholarship fund with the Joint Ministry team. Based on their strong support, he next took the idea to the church body. They too readily embraced the concept. To show the power of God when in His will, Pilgrim contributed $45,000 in November and December toward this new fund. During the year a process for distributing funds and monitoring usage will be developed.

Gearing Up for Africa Mission Trip

Pilgrim's youth have gone on three impressive mission trips. The first trip was to Louisiana; the next two were to Mexico. The youth have set their sights on Africa in 2008. The specific country is yet to be decided. The youth have raised over $6,000 so far and expect to double this amount in 2007. They have always raised sufficient funds and have never ended a trip in debt. They still have loads of work ahead of them. Yet, if they continue past practices, we will wave farewell to them in 2008 as they board the plane for a very long flight to Africa for a magnificent mission to minister and win souls for Christ.

Ministries In Review

Marvelously Sanctified Ministries

Pilgrim is blessed and privileged to have many strong and talented ministries and ministry leaders. They are guided by an inner conviction for excellence in service to our Lord and Savior. Each ministry strives to be faithful and obedient to God's will, not man's will in meeting the needs of His chosen people.

"We continually remember before our God and Father your work produced by faith, your labor prompted by love and your endurance inspired by hope in our Lord Jesus Christ."
— 1 Thessalonians 1:3

Children and Youth Choirs were simply amazing. If you came to Sunday morning service when these choirs were singing, you surely left blessed. The angelic voices of preschoolers to high school students praise the Lord with traditional and contemporary Christian songs. They were busy this year with 11 engagements in and away from Pilgrim. They were a hit at the fourth Annual One Christmas Night. The choirs raised over $2,500 and gave $300 to the Pastor and Wife's Anniversary Celebration. As good stewards, they spent $1,800 less than raised. Accolades are also due the hard work out front and behind the scenes: directors Calvin and Ann Ross, parent helpers, Gwen Rhett, Andrea Bolts and Stacey Guyton and percussionist, Shavin Ross.

Deacons were blessed to add three new Deacons this year, under the leadership of Breakin "BJ" Strickland. This ministry continued to advance the Congregation Driven Ministry through the tribal structure. Tribes are getting individuals and families involved in the church and the church tied into the lives of members. Meeting on fifth Sundays during the Sunday school hour, participation and outcomes have grown. Tribes are primed for great work in 2007.

Facilities Committee had a year of multiple major challenges that under the leadership of Tyrone Robinson were all masterfully overcome. Samples problems fixed were: reoccurring and wasteful water leaks, unsafe and unstable stairs and handrail at the rental unit; raised and broken sidewalk in front and on the side of the church. The committee addressed well overdue upgrades: a new roof over the sanctuary was installed; old lights in the sanctuary were replaced with energy efficient lights; interior of the Education wing was repainted; the elevator was brought up to code.

Family Counseling Staff understands seeking counseling is a sensitive decision. Confidentiality is unerringly honored. Counseling services are provided in a professional setting by faith based and trained staff. If you need individual, couple or family counseling; grief, crisis, or pre-marital counseling, referrals may be made through your Deacon, the Pastor, or church staff. Pilgrim is grateful. Erma Profiro's counseling has attracted no fewer than two other Pilgrim members into the Christian Counseling field.

Home Bible Study under the leadership of Bobbie Arnold, stressed reading and studying the Word for yourself to gain knowledge, understanding and application of God's Word in your everyday life. "For this very reason, make every effort to add to your faith goodness; and to goodness, knowledge", 2 Peter 1:5. Members are expressing a deepening personal walk with the Lord. HBS has finished Warren Wiersbe's, *Be Available*, *Be Committed*, *Be Faithful*, *Be Mature*, and *Be Obedient*. Pastor Ellis's convicting book *The Peter Paradox*, was eagerly studied. During the year, over 135 believers attended 18 HBS groups.

Music, Drama, Fine Arts and Media Team provided another year of inspirational music. The Men in Black Concert, One Christmas Night V, the Fourth Annual Gospel Music & Academic Workshop and over six outside performances were all successful. Enhancements to the ministry were a men's Praise Team, and the First Annual Ministry Fellowship. The Media Team, now part of this ministry, spearheaded acquisition of new equipment, new projection screen computer program, spotlight, and microphones. Dr. Steven Roberts, Reverend Toray Campbell, Fred Howell and Reuben Hill surpassed their previous standards of excellence.

Sunday School Department taught God's Word with the Bible as the base. Women's Classes two and three studied the book of Romans. Young Adults Class studied Your Walk with Christ. The Men's Class examined A Man After God's Own Heart. Couples' Class tackled You Can be The Wife of a Happy Husband. Reverend Campbell, Juanita Guyton, Tynetta Brooks, and Gregory Louis are the newest teachers. In 2006, 416 reliably attended Sunday school along with 70 visitors. Total Sunday school offering was $21,160.

Trustee Board had a stupendous year under the leadership of outgoing chair, Allen Conway. Stewardship Month's theme was "God's 90-10 Blessing Plan". Sermons, Bible study, Sunday School and Tribes all gave focus to getting and staying out of debt. Reverend Campbell stirred sensibilities with his inspiring delivery of two joint adult Sunday School lessons. The highest collection totals were recorded in October and November. Pastor Ellis's preaching/teachings,
and members' generosity, led to a financial breakthrough this year. Pilgrim stepped out on faith and achieved a $1 million annual budget. Praise God.

Usher Boards, both Senior and Junior, attracted new members again this year. The Senior Usher Board was honored to host a Northern District Union Usher Board meeting. The ushers raised $3,335 from their Annual Ushers' Easter Breakfast, Pilgrim Ushers' Annual Day, and several generous love offerings. Larry Croon served as Senior Usher Board president. Junior Ushers are led by Michael and Carmen Green.

Youth Ministry was blessed with a great sense of excitement in 2006. From churches all around the broader Bay Area, 200 teens attended the Annual True Love Waits Teen Conference. Two lock-ins housed 60 youth for prayer, praise, and presentations on youth issues. They played video games, bible trivia, saw movies and of course the pillow fight. Fifty youth went to the Holy Hip-Hop in San Jose and had pizza in Hayward. The youth also enjoyed a Warriors Basketball Game Gospel night at the Oakland Arena. The youth ended 2006, with a trip to Riverside for the California State Youth Conference.

2006 PILGRIM BAPTIST ANNUAL REPORT

Pilgrim Organization, Inc.

History

As you know, in April of 2002, Pilgrim Organization Inc. was incorporated as a California Public Benefit Corporation. This came about out of a desire for Pilgrim Baptist Church to meet more than just the spiritual needs of its members. It was a vision of Pastor Ellis to go outside the walls of the church to meet the physical, emotional and socioeconomic needs of under served members of community in proximity of Pilgrim. POI provides the church financial with the autonomy to impact the community in a mighty way.

Mission

Pilgrim Organization, Inc. is a faith based nonprofit organization established to improve the quality of life for minority and disadvantaged youth and seniors in San Mateo and surrounding Bay Area communities.

Vision

Minority and disadvantaged youth and seniors in San Mateo and surrounding communities are provided the opportunity to sustain a high quality of life through full access to quality education, career development, health, fitness and wellness programs and stable housing.

Pillar (Fundamental Purpose)	Youth	Seniors
Education	• High School Exit Exam • College Admissions Info • College Scholarship Info • Alternative College Info • Parental Involvement	• Contemporary Life Skills • Technology Awareness • Computer Skills • Telecommunication
Career Development	• Job Shadow • Internship • Career Interest Assessment • Volunteer Opportunities	• Changing Careers/Jobs • Retirement Transitions • Skills Assessment • Volunteer Opportunities
Health, Fitness & Wellness	• Prevention Education – Pregnancy, STD's, Drugs • Healthy Lifestyle – Diet and Exercise • Health Risk Awareness – Diabetes, Asthma, Hypertension	• Mental Health – Community Exposure, Outings, Agencies, Sense of Purpose, Peer Gatherings/Meetings • Physical Health – Diet, Exercise, Health Risks
Stable Housing	• Group Home • Transitional Housing	• Community Services • Support Systems • Independent Living

Golf Tournament

On August 19, at the Chuck Corica Golf Complex, twice as many golfers over last year with clubs in hand were ready for a splendid day of fun. And that it was. The first all women's team played with heart. One of the women narrowly missed winning the longest drive prize. The tournament proceeds were $17,485.75. These funds will assist currently enrolled Pilgrim college students and other college-bound students as they strive for advanced levels of education.

Community Grants

POI was most appreciative to receive $10,500 in awards from the Mills-Peninsula Hospital Foundation and the Silicon Valley Community Foundation, formerly known as the Peninsula Community Foundation.

- **Mills-Peninsula Hospital Foundation** awarded POI $7,500. The grant money is to be used to inspire youth to adopt healthy eating and exercise habits. They will be exposed to and trained on healthy alternatives. If successful, the youth will avoid common health risks such as obesity, diabetes, and hypertension.
- **Silicon Valley Community Foundation: Faiths Partnership** granted POI $3,000. The money will go toward helping transitional housing residents improve their lifeskills, job seeking skills and secure a job. Another aspect of the award is that a professional consultant will advise POI in areas such as fundraising, strategic planning, and leadership development. This will enhance the organization's growth.

Annual Walkathon

The **3rd Annual James L. Hutchinson Walkathon and Health Faire** in part was a greater success than the previous two years. POI attributes this to collaborating with member Hope Whipple, who is also the San Mateo Senior Center's director. Hope organized a splendid the health and wellness program. The walkathon attracted participants from the San Mateo community at large. POI wants to continue this partnership with the Senior Center again in 2007.

Stanford Spartan's Concession Stand

Last fall, Pam Sims-Haygood expertly cajoled teens and adults alike into working one of the busiest concession stands at Stanford's new football stadium. With Pam's persistence and caring spirit, 13 to 23 workers showed up for each of the five home games. Although the Spartans had a rough year, winning only one game all season, Pilgrim's youth had an outstanding year, ending the season with $6,808.94 in profit. The money is earmarked for the 2008 Africa Mission trip. Pilgrim has committed to work eight home games in the 2007 fall season.

Financial Statement

Major Incomes	
Golf Tournament	$17,626.75
Mission Trip	$11931.00
Mills Grant Award	$7000.00
Stanford Concession	$6808.94
Contributions	$4865.08
PCF Grant Award	$3000.00
Safeway eScrip	$1251.00
Total Income	**$54,044.77**

Major Expenses	
Scholarship	$11,050.00
Golf Tournament	$5234.70
Mission Trip	$8182.81
California Youth Conference	$3769.88
Total Expenses	**$33,002.39**
Net Ordinary Income	**$21,042.38**

Total Income for Past Five Years

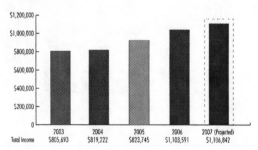

Total Income	2003	2004	2005	2006	2007 (Projected)
	$805,693	$819,222	$823,745	$1,103,591	$1,106,842

Monies coming into Pilgrim in 2006 broke the million dollar threshold for income totaling $1,040,000. This was an 11% increase over 2005 which was also a banner income year at $924,000. Pilgrim held to its proven tradition of stepping out on faith, believing all things are possible and having faith that God will work it out.

2006 PILGRIM BAPTIST ANNUAL REPORT

Major Income Streams

Regular Offering has typically been the largest income source outside of tithes. This time Special Days (8%) and Rental Income (7%) out paced Regular offering (5%) of total income. Scholarship endowment campaign ($65,000) and Church 80th Anniversary Banquet ($12,273), part of Special Days, drove up the percentage.

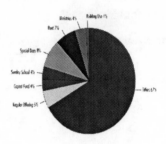

Rental Income

The three rental properties enjoyed full occupancy for most of the year. These investments are measuring up to their potential and beginning to pay off handsomely. The Education Center and sanctuary rental for non-Pilgrim purposes is producing income although not at the same level as the housing units.

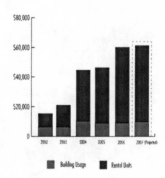

Tithes for 2003 – 2007 Projection

Tithes again this year showed a solid increase. Not only has the amount coming from tithes grown, so has the number of those who now tithe. Tithes represented 67% of Pilgrim's income in 2006 as compared to 66% in 2005. Chief Financial Officer, Woodrow Andrews, expects this trend to continue into 2007 and has projected tithes to increase nearly $30,000. We are truly blessed that such a large portion of the congregation tithes. Our long term goal is to become a fully-tithing church, and we are well on our way toward success – Praise God

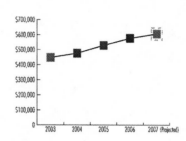

Total Expenses

Pilgrim's most accurate expense projection for 2006 was $1,011,027. By controlling spending, we spent $93,307 less than projected. Again, Pilgrim's expenditures did not exceed the total monies collected. We are grateful to our CFO and his fiscal staff, who have provided exemplary stewardship over Pilgrim's collective assets.

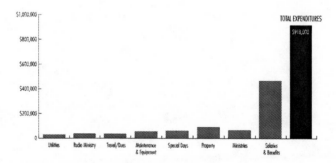

Prepared and Produced by
2006 Annual Report Committee
February 2007

Pilgrim Baptist Church
Reverend Dr. Larry Wayne Ellis, Senior Pastor
217 North Grant Street, San Mateo, CA 94401
Phone: 650-343-5415 • Fax: 650-685-4170
www.pilgrimbcsm.org

The Paradigm of a Tribe

Simeon Tribe

Reverend Dr. Larry Wayne Ellis
Senior Pastor
B.J. Strickland
Chairman, Deacon Ministry
Allen Conway
Chairman, Trustee Ministry

𝔓ilgrim 𝔅aptist 𝔔hurch

217 North Grant Street
San Mateo, California 94401
(650) 343-5415

Mildred Swann
Church Clerk
Tynetta Brooks
Financial Secretary
Woodrow Andrews
Chief Financial Officer

Dear Member:

Grace and peace unto you in the name of our Lord and Savior, Jesus Christ.

I am writing to inform you of our tribe, explain a few aspects of the tribal system within Pilgrim's Congregation-Driven Ministry and invite you to participate in our first churchwide meeting of all twelve tribes on Sunday, April 30th, 2006 @ 9:45 A.M., during the regular time for Sunday School between the 8 and 11 A.M. worship services.

Enclosed you will find a two-page exhibit (#1), entitled "Twelve Tribes of Israel System." This exhibit describes the overall system and answers six of the most frequently asked questions. Another enclosed exhibit (#2), gives you an historic, Biblical view of Simeon, for whom our tribe is named. The third exhibit (#3), lists the 10 ministry leaders within our tribe and summarizes their respective responsibilities. Taken together, these three exhibits provide a foundation for understanding how our tribe fits into the larger tribal system of Pilgrim as well as how we are structured internally to help meet the needs of individual tribe members.

As the scriptural basis for the Tribe of Simeon, I have selected 1 Peter 5:2 to guide our affairs—

> *Feed the flock of God which is among you, taking the oversight thereof, not by constraint, but willingly; not for filthy lucre, but of a ready mind; (KJV)*

> *Be shepherds of God's flock that is under your care, serving as overseers, not because you must, but because you are willing, as God wants you to be; not greedy for money, but eager to serve. (KJV)*

In short, I chose this passage because we have a responsibility to serve and our motivation for serving must stem from love.

As noted above, the initial tribal system meeting will occur on the fifth Sunday in April and we want to ensure that the Tribe of Simeon is well represented. Thus, I am extending this invitation for you to join with other members of our tribe in helping to implement the tribal system and further our spiritual walk. We look forward to seeing you there!

If you have any questions or concerns, please feel free to contact me directly @ (650) 872-2565.

Your Brother in Christ & Tribal Leader
Deacon Willie Sneed

Twelve Tribes of Israel System

DEACONS AND DEACONESSES: B. J. STRICKLAND, CHAIR
Deacons Anderson, Bunn, Campbell, Crump, Jackson, Jones, Louis, Myers, Sneed, Spencer, Strickland

The **Tribal System** is the next step in Pilgrim's longstanding **Congregation Driven Ministry** concept. The purpose of this new system is to help every member feel a part of the body of Christ. It is easy to come to church Sunday after Sunday and yet never really connect to the Pilgrim family. A member may be missing for several weeks before anyone notices. New members join but may soon fall away because there was no one there to nurture this new babe in Christ. The Tribal System is designed to correct problems such as these.

WHAT IS THE BACKGROUND OF THE TRIBAL SYSTEM?

The Tribal System goes back to the days of Jacob whose name God changed to Israel. From this one man came the nation or family of Israel who had twelve sons. From the descendents of these sons came the twelve tribes. Each tribe was accountable for meeting the needs of each family within the clan. Each family was accountable for uplifting the tribal body by teaching each other, meeting family needs, giving support and encouragement, protecting members from harm and celebrating good times.

How will the Tribal System work at Pilgrim?

Deacons are the organizing leaders of the 12 Tribes. Each family has been assigned to a Tribe, there are at least 10 families in each tribe. Each deacon will send a letter to members introducing themselves and will give overview of the system. Next, the deacons will call a one-hour "Gathering" of all families to explain the concept in more detail. Other leaders will be appointed at or before the first Gathering.

What other leaders are needed for each tribe?

Secretary: Take meeting notes and keep records. **Fellowship:** Develop relationships. **Evangelism/Outreach:** Minister to non-Christians. **Discipleship:** Encourage spiritual growth. **Prayer Warrior:** Pray for others. **Women's Missionary:** Mission projects. **Men's Ministry:** Get men involved. **Youth Ministry:** Meet interests of youth. **Music Ministry:** Praise through music. A Trustee and Associate Minister has been/will be assigned to each Tribe.

Who are the Deacon Leaders for the Tribes?

Tribe	Deacon	Tribe	Deacon
Reuben	Sherman Anderson	Simeon	Willie Sneed
Ephraim	Jeff Jackson	Judah	James Campbell
Issachar	B.J. Stickland	Zebulun	Jessie Jones
Dan	Wyner Spencer	Benjamin	Brian Crump
Gad	Daniel Bunn	Asher	Lafayette Myers

How and when will I find out to which Tribe I belong?

Each member will receive a **letter/email** and perhaps a phone call from your deacon, welcoming you and your family into the tribe. The notice will give an overview of the Tribal System with details on your first Gathering. If for some reason you have not received a notice, you may contact any deacon.

What does a Tribal System look like?

Cathy Robinson fashioned **Summer Vacation Bible School** after the Tribal System. Those who attended experienced yesteryear's tribal life. They took part in nightly "Gatherings" in the market place. They learned about the 12 tribes, tribal customs and Jewish worship. They learned about the type of work performed, kind of food eaten and various games played. They carried the flag of their tribes and even dressed in the clothes of those days. **Vacation Bible School** was a superb groundbreaking for our own tribal system today. Pilgrim's Tribes will work together as a unit to meet the needs of both individuals and families. They will be accountable for and to members, will advance spiritual growth and build relationships. They will pray for each other and will, of course, grow in their faith.

"Upon this rock I will build my church and the gates of hell shall not prevail against it."
Matthew 16:13(b)

Tribe of Simeon

<u>Ministry Leaders</u>

Frank Crumb   Evangelism/Outreach

The responsibilities of the Evangelism/Outreach leader include, but are not limited to witnessing to tribe members and their extended family that do not attend church on a regular basis. This person will help new members of the tribe become acclimated into the tribe. He/she will work with Deacon Willie Sneed to ensure that the special needs of the sick and shut-in are met in a timely fashion.

Gerry Ferguson   Secretary

The responsibilities of the Secretary include, but are not limited to taking minutes (notes) and attendance. This person will work closely with the Tribal leaders, monitoring the direction of the Tribe. The Tribe of Simeon Secretary will keep accurate records of tribe members' information such as names, addresses, phone numbers, emails and birth dates. He/she will work with the deaconess in the tribe.

Martha Gray   Sunday School Fellowship

The responsibilities of the Sunday School Fellowship leader include, but are not limited to encouraging members of the tribe to participate in Sunday School, Home Bible Study and other activities of the church. This person will assist Deacon Willie Sneed in the planning and implementing of activities for the tribe of Simeon.

Trina Pierce   Women's Ministry

The responsibilities of the Women's Ministry leader include, but are not limited to involving women members of the tribe in activities that will foster fellowship, Christian growth and maturity. This person will work with Deacon Sneed in encouraging female tribe members' participation in churchwide mission projects. She will also work with the Discipleship and Fellowship leaders.

Mildred Swann   Care Group

The responsibilities of the Care Group leader include being cognizant of the special needs of a Tribe member. She will work with Deacon Sneed in handling special needs with empathy, confidentiality, sensitivity and compassion.

Justin Ellis   Youth Leader

The Youth Ministry Leader's responsibilities include working with all age groups of youth and young adults in the tribe. He/she will encourage young people of the tribe to participate in activities of the church, especially Tuesday nights. He/she will also become familiar with the church youth leaders, choirs, bible study and work with the Fellowship leader to encourage Sunday School attendance.

Marsha Winters   Discipleship

The responsibilities of the Discipleship leader include, but are not limited to keeping members aware and seeking spiritual growth activities both within and outside the church. This person will encourage members to grow in their Christian walk through personal prayer, Bible Study and devotion. She/he will work with the Fellowship leader in providing opportunities/activities that will enhance their Christian growth.

PILGRIM BAPTIST CHURCH
THE TRIBE OF SIMEON

Frank Crumb

Evangelism/Outreach Ministry

1. Haysbert, Allen & Ayanna
2. Howell, Fred
3. Ricks, Edward
4. Tolson, Carlton

Geri Ferguson

Secretary

1. Wagner, Barbara

Martha Gray

Sunday School Fellowship Ministry

1. Bratton, William & Debra
2. Crumb, Frank & Janice
3. Dixon, Dheyanna
4. Levingston, Joyce

Fred Howell

Men's Ministry

1. Jones, Douglas
2. Swann, Willie & Mildred

Deborah Kirk

Tribal Project Ministry

1. Prothro, Erma
2. Spencer, Wyner & Pam & Family

Edwin Mack

Prayer Warriors Ministry

1. Jones, Phelicia
2. Pierce, Trina

Trina Pierce

Women's Ministry

1. Archer, Anyta
2. Ferguson, Geraldine
3. Winters, Marsha—

Mildred Swann

Care Group Ministry

1. Anderson, Sherman
2. Ellis, Justin
3. Kirk, Debbie

Justin Ellis

Youth Ministry

1. Grier, Tiffiney
2. Mack, Edwin & Claire
3. Owens, Larry & Ramunda & Family
4. Wildee, Patricia Pickett

Marsha Winters

Discipleship Ministry

1. Adiwidya, Kira
2. Gray, Yates & Martha
3. Guion, Alene
4. Johnson, Aretha

CDM Training and Workshop Handouts

Joshua 1:1-11
The Congregation Driven Ministry

Title: No one left behind

Mark 6:31-42 (feeding the multitudes)

1. The tribes (God's people) were inclusive:
   A. no one left behind
   B. no one left out

2. The tribes were to walk into their promised land: v. 16
   A. we will do
   B. we will go

3. Failure to follow God's appointed leader was rebellion: v. 17
   A. we will listen
   B. allow God to lead

The biblical basis for The Congregation Driven Ministry

Joshua was a disciple of Moses. A disciple is a focused learner
God's command is to make disciples Matt. 28:18-20

1. Sunday School ... Second Tim. 2: 15
2. Home Bible Study ... Acts 2:41-47 (Apostle's teaching) 12
3. Ministry ... First Corinthians 12:12-27
4. Full body tithing ... Philippians 4:19

The entire congregation's needs are met and the community is changed! God gets glory.

The Congregation Driven Ministry

What is it?

The **Congregation Driven Ministry is** a church model that is Christ centered and bible based. Its vision is to grow a ministry that is a fully functioning faith based fellowship.

Each group fulfills its bible sanctioned work:
1. Pastor cast the vision … (Hosea 4:6, Proverbs 29: 18, Eph. 4: 11:16)
2. The role of the staff is to promote the vision
3. Ministers/evangelist support the pastor by practicing their gifts in the body (2 Timothy :2, 2 Corinthians 4:1-2)
4. Deacons support the pastor by caring for the congregation (Acts 6)
5. Trustees fund the vision by developing a stewardship ministry that the congregation can understand and support (1st Corinthians 4: 1-2)
6. The congregation commits to Christ, the word of God and the use of spiritual gifts in ministry (Acts 2:42-47)

It affirms that each member has:
- Unique personality
- Spiritual gifting
- Personal story/journey that has value
- Call to fulfill

Stages of Growth:
- Salvation
- Preparation
- Responsibility
- Evaluation

T E A M (review) together-each-achieves-more
- Trust
- Encouragement
- Affirmation
- Motivation

TWELVE TRIBES OF ISRAEL

The Nation of Israel was organized according to tribes for several reasons:

1. It was an effective way to manage and govern a large group.

2. It made dividing the promised land easier.

3. It was part of their culture and heritage (people were not known by last name, but by their family, clan and tribe).

4. It made it easier to keep detailed genealogies and genealogies were the only way to prove membership in God's chosen nation.

5. It made travel much more efficient. The people followed the tribe's standard (a kind of flag) and thus they stayed together, which kept them from getting lost.

Simeon

Simeon was the second-born son of Jacob/Israel, after Reuben and before Levi (see Levites). His mother was Leah. Simeon was fierce toward his enemies e.g. he and his full-brother Levi (Jacob's twelve sons were born by his two wives, Leah and Rachel and two Concubines, Bilhah and Zilpah—see Children of Jacob) slaughtered Hamor and the Shechemites after the violation of Simeon and Levi's sister Dinah. His loyalty to his family was at times opportunistic, e.g., he joined with his brothers in selling their brother Joseph (see Coat of Many Colors) to the Ishmaelites who took him to Egypt (Genesis 37:12-28). For that, he was later, after Joseph's rise to power in Egypt, temporarily held as a hostage (Genesis 42:24). After the Israelites crossed the Jordan into the Promised Land, the offspring of Simeon, the tribe of Simeon, were allotted the territory in the south of the land promised to the descendants of Abraham, Isaac and Jacob, which included the cities of Beersheba (see also Dan to Beersheba) and Arad (see also Bible Places).

<u>Tribal Lands</u>

www.keyway.ca

The birth of Leah's first four children, which included Simeon:

"And Leah conceived and bore a son and she called his name Reuben; for she said, "Because the Lord has looked upon my affliction; surely now my husband will love me." She conceived again and bore a son and said, "Because the Lord has heard that I am hated, he has given me this son also"; and she called his name Simeon. Again she conceived and bore a son and said, "Now this time my husband will be joined to me, because I have borne him three sons"; therefore his name was called Levi. And she conceived again and bore a son and said, "This time I will praise the Lord"; therefore she called his name Judah." (Genesis 29:32-35 RSV)

Simeon and Levi's vengeance on Hamor, for which later their father Jacob vilified them on his death bed:

"On the third day, when they were sore, two of the sons of Jacob, Simeon and Levi, Dinah's brothers, took their swords and came upon the city unawares and killed all the males. They slew Hamor and his son Shechem with the sword and took Dinah out of Shechem's house and went away." (Genesis 34:25-26 RSV)

"Simeon and Levi are brothers; weapons of violence are their swords. O my soul, come not into their council; O my spirit, be not joined to their company; for in their anger they slay men and in their wantonness they hamstrung oxen. Cursed be their anger, for it is fierce; and their wrath, for it is cruel! I will divide them in Jacob and scatter them in Israel" (Genesis 49:5-7 RSV)

The first descendants of Simeon:

"The sons of Simeon: Jemuel, Jamin, Ohad, Jachin, Zohar and Shaul, the son of a Canaanite woman; these are the families of Simeon." (Exodus 6: 15 RSV)

After the Exodus, the Simeonites camped on the south side of the Tabernacle in the wilderness between Reuben and Gad (see The Camp):

"On the south side shall be the standard of the camp of Reuben by their companies, the leader of the people of Reuben being Elizur the son of Shedeur, his host as numbered being forty-six thousand five hundred. And those to encamp next to him shall be the tribe of Simeon, the leader of the people of Simeon being Shelumiel the son of Zurishaddai, his host as numbered being fifty-nine thousand three hundred. Then the tribe of Gad, the leader of the people of Gad being Eliasaph the son of Reuel, his host as numbered being forty-five thousand six hundred and fifty." (Numbers 2:10-15 RSV)

After their entry into the Promised Land, the tribe of Simeon was allotted the land south of Judah (see map above):

"The second lot came out for Simeon, for the tribe of Simeon, according to its families; and its inheritance was in the midst of the inheritance of the tribe of Judah ... together with all the villages round about these cities as far as Baalathbeer, Ramah of the Negeb. This was the inheritance of the tribe of Simeon according to its families. The inheritance of the tribe of Simeon formed part of the territory of Judah; because the portion of the tribe of Judah was too large for them, the tribe of Simeon obtained an inheritance in the midst of their inheritance." (Joshua 19: 1,8-9 RSV)

Fact Finder: Will 12,000 from the tribe of Simeon be among the 144,000? Revelation 7:4-8

The Daily Bible Study: http://www.keyway.ca

An Annual Report Paradigm

Pilgrim Baptist Church

2005 Annual Report

North Grant Street
San Mateo, CA 94401
650.343.5415
Reverend Dr. Larry Wayne Ellis, Senior Pastor

Pastor's Message to the Church

Date with Destiny

We will celebrate eighty years in ministry this year! The Lucas family had a dream of a church in San Mateo. We are the ful-fillment of that vision. Many brothers and sisters have graced this ministry through the years. We are a multi-staffed Church blessed with gifted lay and clergy leaders. As senior pastor, it is my responsibility to give leadership to this church family. I believe that God has prepared us to do a God size work this year! I sense that the Lord has Pilgrim on a mission. We have a date with destiny. All things are ready. We must seize this great opportunity to turn our "world" upside-down for Christ, or is it right side up? Our community is in need of the spiritual direction that God has called us to provide. Our new staff in the finance, music and discipleship ministries will enhance our ability to function effectively. With over twenty home bible studies and ministries, we can provide spiritual nourishment from the cradle to the convalescent home. Our new Wednesday evening service will fill a void in the lives of those members who work on Sunday. Moreover, it will bless many who sense a need for more in their spiritual life. Let us support with our prayers and presence.

I am asking that we accept the new "Tribe" ministry as an extension of The Congregation Driven Ministry. We can ensure that every member who desires to be a part of the fellowship will find his or her place. I thank God for each member. I praise him for allowing me this awesome privilege to serve Pilgrim. You are a great people who serve a great God! We have come this far by faith. Let us all work together to make this year one of the greatest years in our illustrious history. We stand on his promise ..."upon this rock I will build my church and the gates of hell shall not prevail against it." *Matthew 16:13(b)*

In Christ together,

Larry Ellis

Dr. Larry W. Ellis, Senior Pastor

Chief Financial Officer

Pilgrim has become a church with a million dollar annual budget. Pastor Ellis and the leadership team recognized that such a budget required the dedicated help of an experienced and knowledgeable person. The role of a Chief Financial Officer (CFO) was developed and recruited to ensure that our church finances are managed thoroughly. **Woody Andrews** was a natural pick for the job. He has served in various financial roles during his membership at Pilgrim. Woody has voluntarily drafted the annual budget for many years. He is a past Chair of the Trustee Ministry. He is vice president of Pilgrim Organization, Inc. His corporate experience and education have also prepared Woody for the role. We are blessed that he is here to oversee and advance Pilgrim's financial affairs.

Q: Whom does the CFO report to?

The CFO reports to Pastor Ellis and works closely with the Trustee and Deacon Ministries.

Q: What are the duties of the CFO?

The CFO oversees and is accountable for all financial and business matters of the church. He leads the development of our annual church budget, tracks the budget, reviews and analyzes weekly financial reports, reviews and approves weekly staff payroll, and manages all bank accounts.

Q: Is that all?

No. The CFO is also responsible for finding key opportunities to fund Pastor's mission in partnership with the Trustees. In conjunction with the Trustees, he sets short and long-term goals and helps reduce church debt. He works closely with the tax accountant for tax and other filings. He ensures compliance with applicable government regulations. Finally, he is the link between Pilgrim Church and Pilgrim Organization Inc.

Q: How has the CFO position made a difference?

The CFO updated the church software. This made tracking and reporting on church financial matters faster and cleaner. The new system automated membership recordkeeping and ad hoc reporting; weekly and monthly reports were standardized; the payroll and budget process was streamlined and he eliminated banking redundancies. Woody has two new projects underway. One is to develop and refine church processes and compile the data in a church manual.

Pilgrim Baptist Church Financial Report

1. **Total Income**

   In 2005, Pilgrim's **overall income** was <u>$902,586</u>. That was an $26,484
   increase over last year ($819,222). We are so grateful to our congregation
   and ministries for making this possible. Pilgrim's faith based projection for
   income in 2006 is **$1,011,027**.

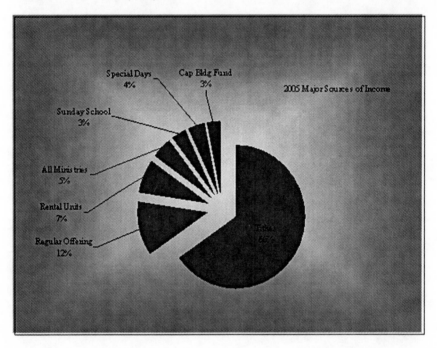

2. Major Income Sources

Regular Offering again was the largest source of income outside of tithes. Rental Income was the next largest income stream at $55,000.00 for 2005.

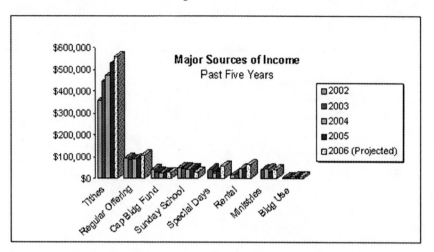

3. Tithes

There was a **modest but steady growth** in tithes again. Tithes represented **66% of all income** in 2005 for a total of **$528,766**, an increase over 2005. We are mightily blessed that so many members faithfully tithe.

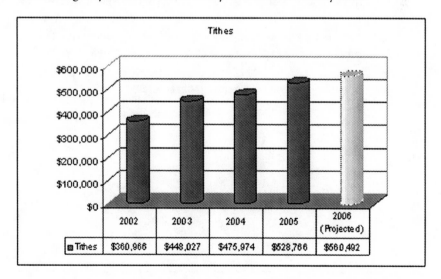

4. Total Expenses

Pilgrim's best projection for 2006 expense is **$1,011,027.** You can see below how expenses have tracked with income since 2003, which is common for other years. Through the years, Pilgrim has continued to keep spending under control.

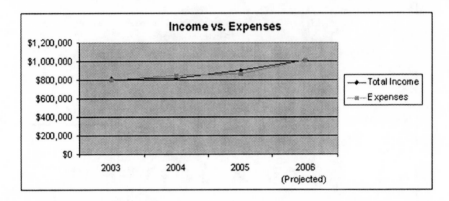

Whether it's a small non-profit or a major corporation, **Salary & Benefits** is typically the largest line item in any organization's budget. In many instances, half or more of the budget goes toward Salary & Benefits. Pilgrim's Salary & Benefits however, is **less than half of our budget.** That is a real blessing.

Pilgrim's next largest expense is **Ministries expenses.** Pilgrim ministries incur costs as they do ministry work and most often are fortunate to annually raise funds to meet their annual ministry expenses. Occasionally the church will cover nominal ministry expenses that exceed annual ministry fundraising.

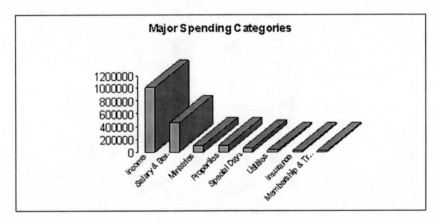

Remembering Those Called Home in 2005

"Precious in the sight of the Lord is the death of his saints. O Lord ... you have freed me from my chains" Psalm 116:15-16

He will wipe every tear from their eyes. There will be no more death or mourning or crying or pain, for the old order of things have passed away". Rev. 21:4

Essie Bernice Bunn, Feb 3, 1925–Dec. 15, 2005
She united with Pilgrim in 1998. Sister Bunn was a true servant of the Lord and loved doing whatever she could for him and the church. She was steadfast in her faith until the very end. Sister Bunn's favorite saying was, "Just have the faith of a mustard seed."

Renaldo (Bo Bo) Groves, Dec 3, 1950–Dec. 29, 2005
Renaldo was Joseph and Barbara Groves' oldest child of six. He was christened at Pilgrim and attended church here through the years. He was employed by the U. S. Postal Data Center for many years. Renaldo considered Pilgrim as his home.

Michelle Holland, Feb. 9, 1960–July 23, 2005
She gave her life to God on March 1, 2004 at Pilgrim. Michelle was proof that it does not matter how long but how strong a Christian woman you are. She served on the Usher Board, attended Women's Sunday School Class #2, and participated in the "Sista-to-Sista Women of Christ" Retreat. You could always find Michelle on Wednesday nights at Prayer Meeting. She loved the Lord and acknowledged the changes <u>he</u> made in her life.

Karen Lisa (Mickey) Johnson-Patterson, Feb 14, 1959–April 12, 2005
Karen completed New Members Training just weeks before her death. Karen had a big smile and enjoyed being with her family, friends, and grandchildren. She loved to shop for shoes and handbags. Karen was the only girl of six children. She was so proud to be in the arms of our Savior and a member of Pilgrim.

Solomon McCollough, Jan. 3, 1919–Sept. 8, 2005

Sol was a long-time member of Pilgrim. He served as Trustee Ministry chair and sang with the Male Chorus. Sol energetically served at Pilgrim until his illness would no longer permit him to do so. He was a member of the US Army for 23 year. He was a manager at the California Automobile Association for 19 years. Sol managed the San Mateo NAACP Credit Union for many years. He was vice president of NAACP. He was also a member of San Francisco Commonwealth Club. Sol lived an active and full life.

Paul Richard Phillips, Dec. 28, 1920–March 27, 2005
Paul confessed Christ as his Savior in his latter years and attended Pilgrim reliably until his death. He retired from Rector Cadillac in Burlingame as a journeyman mechanic. He received the coveted Honors Veteran's Badge from the Grand Lodge of International Association of Machinists and Aerospace Workers for over 20 years of loyal service.

Deacon John Prothro, Sr. Oct. 27, 1934–Sept. 7, 2005
Deacon Prothro joined Pilgrim Baptist Church under the leadership of the late Rev. John Cooper. He quickly became involved in church ministry and stayed active for over 25 years until he became ill in late 2004, just weeks after his 70th birthday.

He served on the Senior Usher Board, Deacon Board, and Benevolent Committee. He was a Sunday School teacher and ultimately became Superintendent. He greatly enjoyed serving as Pastor Larry Ellis' armor bearer. He found much joy in traveling with Pastor throughout the Bay Area and the State for revivals and special events. Deacon Prothro and his wife, Erma, were among the first to open their home for Home Bible Study and have kept it open continuously.

"Pop" as he was known by his children and "Papa" as his five grandchildren called him, was a faithful and obedient servant of the Lord. Young and senior members alike and those in the community held Deacon Prothro in high regard. He was a dapper dresser and a "Tiger Woods wannabe". He also found time to take on several leadership roles within his Foster City community. Our memory of Deacon will be that of a model Christian and a faithful and obedient servant. We find peace in knowing that our Father in heaven loved him best and wanted him home to be at his side.

There will be no more night. They will not need the light of a lamp or the light of the sun, for the Lord God will give them light. And they will reign for ever and ever." Rev. 22:5

New Membership

Jesus replied, *"Everyone who drinks of this water will be thirsty again, but whoever drinks the water I give him will never thirst."* John 4:13. During 2005, **128 new members** accepted the "living water" by joining the body of Christ at Pilgrim. Those believers who joined on the first Sunday of the year were **Phyliss Greenridge** and **Connie Miller**. On the last Sunday of the year, we welcomed in **Brain Crump, Amy Ellen Feldman, Arthur Hunter, Charles Clifford Lewis, Dawn Rosales, Carol Salazar** and **Carolina Serrano**. We thank these all members for accepting *"a spring of water welling up to eternal life."* Our goal at Pilgrim is to keep our arms of protection around each of them and help them all grow into matured Christians.

2005 New Membership Rolls

	Baptism	Christian Experience	Restoration	Total
January	5	7	1	13
February	9	3	2	14
March	4	5	1	10
April	8	3	0	11
May	1	2	0	3
June	5	0	0	5
July	6	4	0	10
August	2	5	1	8
September	2	3	1	6
October	13	16	2	31
November	1	2	3	6
December	4	1	6	11

Pilgrim Church Ministries Highlights

HOME BIBLE STUDY: BOBBIE ARNOLD, CHAIR

The idea behind Home Bible Study is to provide a common place where the shy and the outgoing, the babe and the matured, the skeptic and the devout, Christian and non-Christian can learn together, practice living a reflection of Jesus Christ's life.

Home Bible Study Mission is to reach, teach, make disciples, build relationships, and evangelize. The basic format is small confidential and non-threatening study groups (or cells) developing together with Jesus at the center.

Last year, Home Bible Study cells studied books by Warren W. Wiersbe. The first book was BE AVAILABLE, then BE COMMITTED, and the last for the year was BE MATURE.

Special recognition and loving gratitude go out to the **22 hosts and hostesses** who graciously lead a study cell. Those honorable and faithful people are listed below.

Sister Bobbie Arnold *"The Pauline Crew"*	Rev. & Sis. Tion Boxton *"The Heralds of Truth"*	Sister Tynetta Brooks *"Our Circle of Love #2"*
Dea. & Sis Dan Bunn *"The Wayfarers"*	Dea. & Sis. John Campbell *"The Disciples #2"*	Rev. & Sis. Mat Coker *"Tribe of Judah"*
Bro. & Sis. Allen Conway *"Paul's Pilgrims"*	Dea. & Sis. Brian Crump *"East Bay Soldiers for Christ"*	Sister Lenita Ellis *"The Faith Walkers"*
Sis. Joanne Griffin *"Seekers of the Word"*	Sisters Guyton & Wilberforce *"Spiritual Soldiers"*	Bro. & Sis. Raymond Hall *"Jesus Seekers"*
Dea. & Sis. Jessie Jones *"Our Circle of Love #1"*	Bro. Dennis Mays *"The Berean's Noble Way"*	Sister Erma Prothro *"Habakkuk"*
Bro. & Sis. Jeff Prothro *"Shadrach, Meshach, Abednego Crew"*	Bro. Kent Reese *"The Disciples #2"*	Deacon Wyner Spencer *"Heaven Bound Warriors"*
Rev. & Sis. Lonnie Wallace *"Messengers of the Cross"*	Sisters Wheeler & Myers *"Paul's Christian Band"*	Bro. & Sis. Thurman White *"The Revelators"*
	Sister Marsha Winters *"Esther Saints"*	

Trustee: Allen Conway, Chair
Trustees Andrews, Bolts, Briscoe, Emery, Lucas, Merida, Robinson, Myers, Prothro, Shoffner, Watkins, White

Trustees stepped out on faith again in 2005 to undertake matters that affect not only the success of Pilgrim but also impacts the lives of our Pilgrim members. Here is a short list of accomplishments for the year.

- Trustees expanded its rolls by bring on **Janyce Prothro** and **Ron Bolts** after they completed extensive training. Both quickly got involved in all trustee duties. What a blessing to have such well-equipped new members in service.

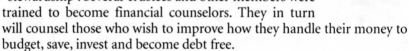

- **Good $ense** money management program was launched. Its purpose is to help members take control over their finances, a way of expanding their personal "stewardship". Several Trustees and other members were trained to become financial counselors. They in turn will counsel those who wish to improve how they handle their money to budget, save, invest and become debt free.

- Pilgrim was graced with another **successful Stewardship Month**. The theme was "**Time, Talent and Treasure—Giving Thanks by using our Gifts for God's Glory**".
  - o In past years, financial giving was the focus; this year the focus was on giving of our **time** and **spiritual gifts** in ministry, not just giving of our treasures.
  - o The new litany was introduced and will be repeated on each 5th Sunday 2006.
  - o The Ministry Faire was incorporated in Stewardship Month for the first time.
  - o **Thirty-one new members** joined Pilgrim in October, the most of any other month. Harvest Sunday, the first Sunday in November, resulted in a blessed offering of **$42,375,** a 32% increase over 2004 Harvest Sunday. Capital Giving Campaign and tithe pledges also rose during Stewardship Month.

- The trustees continued to strengthen spiritually through quarterly Bible Study Meetings. This is time set aside to gather in a member's home to study, pray and fellowship.

Pilgrim Baptist Church enjoyed a bountiful year in 2005. Our prayer for the church and our membership is that, God will continue to "*throw open the floodgates of heaven and pour out so much blessing, that [we] shall not have room enough to receive*". Malachi 3:10

WOMEN'S FELLOWSHIP MINISTRY: JENNIFER BUNN, CHAIR
Retreat Committee: Eleanor William-Curry, Vanderler Ellis, Gertrude Franklin,
Bernetha Hall, Artise Hardy, Charlotte Jackson, Aretha Johnson, Dylan Louis,
Roedell Myers, LaTanya Ross, Pamela Spencer, Jackie Strickland, Jackie Watkins,
Trena Watson, Eileen White

1st Annual Women's Fellowship Retreat

SIS AS

Sisters Inspired Saved Together & Acknowledging Our Savior
PILGRIM BAPTIST CHURCH

"SISTA-TO-SISTA, **Women of Christ: Looking at what is Real**"
Redwood Glen, Loma Mar, California

Friday Evening, April 22

First there was registration, orientation, saying, "Hi" to so many familiar and new faces, getting settled in our rooms and that delicious dinner. Then the "sistas" geared up for a weekend pregnant with reformation, consecration, inspiration, confession, and rededication. The weekend indeed <u>delivered a brand new sense of self</u> from an abundance of discovering, laughing, crying, growing, purging, praying, bonding, and experiencing the ever presence of our Lord, Christ Jesus.

LaTanya Ross was the weekend's first speaker. Her message, "Lord, Help Me with Me", set the tone and freed us up to earnestly be our self. It was powerful!

Can you believe—we actually had a **Pajama Party?** Some of those PJ's were a sight to be seen. Did you hear about the games—cotton ball pick-up, potato-between-the-knees run, musical chairs? Juanita and Labrina Guyton were the last two competing for the last chair. Daughter won but gave the prize to mother with a hug, *how sweet.*

Saturday, April 23

A little rain did not stop our early morning walk, our exercises, nor prayers or meditation. After a big country breakfast, we were off to our workshops. **First**

Lady Patricia Perkins of First Baptist Church (Pittsburg, CA) examined **"Relationships"**. She had us look at the purpose of sista-to-sista relationships, how to nurture them and how to recover from past hurts that strain present relationships. **First Lady Rachelle Smith** of Grace Cathedral Community Church (San Leandro, CA) "told-it-like-it-was" in her workshop on **"Communications"**. She ventured that, "We are a piece of work which in turn affects our communication." She made it clear that our communications with one another is a direct reflection of our relationship with God. Lady Smith was so real, that at times we just had to say "ouch". She gave us practical aids to improve our communications. It was then up to us—with God's help.

During the evening session, Pilgrim's own **Sister Jackie Campbell** led an exchange of ideas to keep the momentum going and staying connected once the retreat was over. Oh yes, we must remember the much-practiced praise dance, what a delight. A spiritual highlight of the evening was the **Fireside Session**. This was time set aside to reflect on our blessings and to release burdens we had written down on paper. We purged ourselves of those burdens by casting the paper into a fire and symbolically lifting them up to the Lord for him to handle. Finally, after more singing, praying, sharing and praising, we were at peace and ready for rest.

Sunday Morning, April 24

Very early Sunday morning, after packing the car, it was time to return home. Around 7:00 a.m. we arrived at Pilgrim to a home cooked breakfast prepared and served by the men. At 8:00 a.m., wearing purple T-shirts, the SISTA's regally marched into the sanctuary ready for service. We proclaimed the retreat an astounding victory because God was boldly present throughout the weekend. We gave thanks and praise.

Sisters Inspired Saved Together & Acknowledging Our Savior
PILGRIM BAPTIST CHURCH

YOUTH MISSION: Rev. Johnie Thompson and John & Julie Brown, Leaders
Participating Youth: David Williams, Tyrus Lewis, Jeffrey Jackson, Danielle Hill, Dawn Simpson, Dominic Pittman, Nichole Paulson, Ian Yoshimoto, Anthony Mace, Shaylona Wheeler

In June of 2005, the Pilgrim Youth Mission Team embarked on a life-changing experience to Vincente Guerrero, Baja, Mexico. Pilgrim teamed with **Youth With A Mission** and three other churches to build houses for needy families. The youth did an amazing job working together measuring and cutting boards, nailing and painting.

Ten youth and three adults, and the Youth Missions Team left early Sunday morning, flying to San Diego to meet up with the other team members. In San Diego, we loaded the luggage and 13 mini-vans started the five-hour caravan into Mexico. The drive became adventurous as we travel a narrow two-lane highway.

The Mission Trip
Vincente Guerrero, Baja, Mexico

Pilgrim had such a positive impact at the Mission and in the community that we were honored to be only the second group ever to be asked back to the Mission. So Pilgrim will be back in Vincente Guerrero in 2006 anxious to be blessed and eager to bless others.

With donations from the youth and using the remaining food money from the trip, we were able to bless the family with a set of bunk beds, queen bed, bed sheets, curtains and two weeks worth of groceries. Before we left our family, each one of us prayed over the keys, blessing the family.

Pilgrim, the only African-American group, taught the other churches what praise and worship was all about. Taking it one step further, Rev. Thompson preached a spirit-filled message. Pilgrim was so inspiring that we were invited to lead worship at a local church. When Rev. Thompson started preaching, the pastor of the local church started translating. It was a translation like none other.

MUSIC, DRAMA & FINE ARTS MINISTRY: DR. *STEVEN E. ROBERTS, MINISTER OF MUSIC* -- *Children's Choir, Drama Guild, Inspiration Choir, Male Chorus, Mass Choir, Praise Dancers, Praise & Worship Team, Women's Choir, Youth Choir*

Year of Successes:

♪ Featured **new soloists and vocal groups** every 5ᵗʰ Sunday

♪ Hosted the **Nor Cal Gospel Music Workshop of America Choir** in concert

♪ Inspirational Choir performed at:

- Pastor Campbell's 28ᵗʰ Anniversary at Mt. Zion Baptist
- Macedonia Church of God in Christ 65ᵗʰ Anniversary
- 65ᵗʰ Annual California State Baptist Convention
- Soul Stroll VIP Banquet, Burlingame Sheraton Hotel

♪ Women's Chorus took part in

Annual Four Seasons Tea

♪ **Torey Campbell** joined the

music team as the Assistant Minister of Music

♪ **Third Annual Pre-Celebration Musical** for First Lady and Pastor's Anniversary

♪ New **instruments and equipment** now ensure performance and sound quality

♪ Third Annual **Men in Black Concert** enjoyed enormous success

♪ **"One Christmas Night, IV"** combined performances by the Drama Guild, Praise Dancers, the Children's and Youth choirs, and a special Celebration Choir

♪ Presented Gospel Pioneer awards to nine for 50+ years of gospel music

♪ Sponsored **educational and independent performances** to underwrite expenses

Psalms 100
1 Make a joyful noise unto the Lord all ye lands. 2 Serve the Lord with gladness: come before his presence with singing. 3 Know ye that the Lord he is God: it is he that hath made us, and not we ourselves; we are his people, and the sheep of his pasture. 4 Enter into his gates with thanksgiving, and into his courts with praise: be thankful unto him, and bless his name. 5 For the Lord is good; his mercy is everlasting; and his truth endureth to all generations.

A Budget Paradigm

Income

4000 · INCOME

4010 · Benevolent	9,080.82	8,500.00	7,861.26	8,097.10
4015 · Building Fund	9,018.39	9,200.00	9,714.17	10,005.60
4020 · Public Offering	14,314.15	14,750.00	14,517.50	14,953.00
4025 · Tithes	475,974.01	490,000.00	528,766.24	560,492.00
4030 · Regular Offering	88,468.07	91,122.00	100,445.21	106,472.00
4035 · Building Income	10,250.00	10,320.00	8,845.00	9,110.35
4050 · Sunday School Offering	41,779.25	43,260.00	28,585.87	29,443.45
4250 · Rent -A	18,547.92	21,000.00	15,750.00	21,500.00
4251 Deposit B	125.00	0.00	500.00	0.00
4255 · Rent C	6,621.00	20,400.00	21,334.50	20,400.00
4256 · Deposit -D	1,500.00	0.00	0.00	0.00
4257 · Rent E	17,900.00	18,000.00	8,990.00	21,500.00
4 · Wednesday Night Service				12,000.00
4000 · INCOME	12,751.46	5,000.00	21,643.12	5,000.00
Total 4000 · INCOME	**706,330.07**	**731,552.00**	**766,952.87**	**818,973.50**

4002 · MINISTRIES INCOME

4001 POI	2,319.00	0.00	700.00	0
4040 · Calendar	5,339.00	4,200.00	1,450.00	3666.8
4041 · Counseling Services	3,257.00	3,937.00	421.20	1500
4045 · Deacons Ministry- World Vision	0.00	3,500.00	0.00	
4046 · Deacons/Deaconess/Trustees Inc				
4047 · Deacons	640.00	720.00	704.00	725
4048 · Deaconess Income	350.00	1,200.00	205.00	211
4049 · Trustees Inc	326.50	500.00	0.00	0
Total 4046 · Deacons/Deaconess/Trustees Inc	**1,316.50**	**2,420.00**	**909.00**	**936.00**
4052 · Drama Ministry	80.00	0.00	0.00	0
4053 · Media Ministry			0.00	
4053 · Media Ministry	2,879.50	2500.00	2,209.00	5000
Total 4053 · Media Ministry	**2,879.50**	**2,500.00**	**2,209.00**	**5,000.00**
4062 · Men's Fellowship Income				0
4066 · Music Department	15,857.47	20,750.00	8,565.99	12000
4091 · Pastor's Auxiliary	4,710.00	5,000.00	5,003.71	9271
4224 · Vacation Bible School	676.00	750.00	0.00	0
4114 · Singles/Couples Ministry			0.00	0
4115 · Singles		0.00	0.00	0
4117 · Couples		5,000.00	2,578.95	2656
Total 4114 · Singles/Couples Ministry	**0.00**	**5,000.00**	**2,578.95**	**2,656.00**
4230 · Usher's Income	4,819.00	3,693.00	3,833.69	4691
4223 Nursery				
4247 · Women's Fellowship Income				
4248 · Women Fellow. Mission Offering	0.00	0.00	0.00	0
4247 · Women's Fellowship Income	950.00	2,000.00	709.00	730.00
Total 4247 · Women's Fellowship Income	**950.00**	**2,000.00**	**709.00**	**730.00**

	4249 · Adult Inspirational Ministry	871.00	2,000.00	0
Total 4002 MINISTRIES INCOME		43,074.47	55,000.00	26,380.54	40,450.80

4004 · SPECIAL DAYS INCOME

4072 · Special Offering	2,400.72	1,000.00	1,078.00	1,000.00
4090 · Special Day	5,284.95	5,500.00	13,207.91	13,604.00
4100 · Church Anniversary	4,873.00	5,000.00	3,924.00	12,000.00
4101 · Church Banquet	0.00	0.00	0.00	15,000.00
4210 · Spring Revival	3,241.02	3,300.00	2,948.68	3,037.00
4211 · Fall Revival	2,264.01	2,300.00	2,821.87	2,881.00
4212 · Harvest Gift	5,520.00	6,000.00	8,961.00	9,230.00
Total 4004 · SPECIAL DAYS INCOME	**23,583.70**	**23,100.00**	**32,941.46**	**56,752.00**

4006 · MISCELLANEOUS

4095 · Miscellaneous Income	0.00	0.00	0.00	
4006 · MISCELLANEOUS	0.00	0.00	560.00	500
Total 4006 · MISCELLANEOUS	**0.00**	**0.00**	**560.00**	**500.00**

4016 · Capital Bldg Fund	24,636.00	30,000.00	26,558.00	27,355.00

4042 · Donations

4043 · Donations (Flowers) Income	150.00	250.00	250.00	335.00
4042 · Donations	1,045.00	1,100.00	325.00	438.00
40 Youth Training and Development (Restricted)				8,000.00
4111 · Hurricane relief			7,986.50	2000
4235 · Scholarship Donation	252.00	0.00	130.00	
Total 4042 · Donations	**1,447.00**	**1,350.00**	**8,691.50**	**10,773.00**

4056 · W. C. Sample Scholarship	0.00	0.00	0.00	0.00
4060 · Home Bible Study	2,791.70	4,500.00	2,981.74	4,500.00
4215 · Radio Ministry	5,387.50	5,100.00	8,753.11	9,000.00
4216 · Travel & Ent Income	0.00	0.00	0.00	
4240 · Vending Machines	1,356.00	1,500.00	1,075.00	1,085.00
4059 · Women's Retreat			11,299.50	11,638.00
4246 · Men Retreat	6,085.00	8,000.00	9,505.52	10,500.00

4261 · Youth Department Income

4069 · Youth Choir		0.00	1,265.00	0.00
4223 · Youth - Nursery	50.00	0.00	0.00	0.00
4261 · Youth Department Income	4,331.37	16,000.00	5,622.06	19,500.00
Total 4261 · Youth Department Income	**4,381.37**	**16,000.00**	**6,887.06**	**19,500.00**

Total Income	**819,222.50**	**876,102.00**	**902,586.30**	**1,011,027.30**

Expense

6040 · MINISTRIES EXPENSES

6125 · Calendar Expenses	3,991.87	4,200.00	3,839.91	3,955.11
6127 · Counseling Ministry Expenses	1,092.82	1,200.00	0.00	0.00
6153 · Deaconess/Women's Fellowship	0.00	0.00	0.00	0.00
6155 · Deaconess Expenses	417.86	1,200.00	169.74	201.00
6461 · Women's Retreat Expenses	671.21	2,000.00	11,445.27	11,638.00
6460 · Women's Fellowship			708.13	760.00
6153 · Deaconess/Women's Fellowship		0.00	0.00	0
Total 6153 · Deaconess/Women's Fellowship	**1,089.07**	**3,200.00**	**12,323.14**	**12,599.00**

6154 · Trustees	1,995.78	1,800.00	343.37	268.50
6157 · Deacons	349.40	300.00	0.00	250.00
6156 · Drama Ministry	793.80	425.00	0.00	0.00
6158 · Media Ministry	2,166.85	2,500.00	2,705.15	2,786.00
6245 · Music Department Expenses	6,390.04	9,150.00	7,402.99	5,000.00
6249 · Pastor's Auxiliary Expenses	634.87	1,000.00	5,003.71	7,987.00
6285 · Evangelism/Radio Ministry Exp	28,365.50	28,690.00	39,043.11	41,200.00
6335 · Sunday School Expenses	2,604.16	3,000.00	5,108.37	5,196.00
6465 · Seniors	3,395.83	4,000.00	0.00	4,500.00
6560 · Home Bible Study Books	4,062.79	4,500.00	3,200.04	4,500.00
6645 · Usher's Auxiliary	2,823.52	2,475.00	1,985.74	2,510.00
6660 · Youth Department	4,831.32	16,000.00	3,227.87	19,500.00
6248 · Youth Choir			627.85	
6662 · Children Church			1,649.77	2,000.00
6678 · Hotdog Sunday			1,150.19	1,045.00
6825 · Adult Inspirational Ministry	785.27	1,000.00	0.00	0.00
6830 · Singles/Couples			0.00	
6831 · Singles	0.00	0.00	200.00	200.00
6832 · Couples	1,021.76	5000.00	5,050.18	2,656.00
Total 6830 · Singles/Couples	1,021.76	5,000.00	5,250.18	2,856.00
Total 6040 · MINISTRIES EXPENSES	66,394.63	88,440.00	92,861.39	116,152.61
6043 · SPECIAL DAYS EXPENSES				
6145 · Church Anniversary Expense	1,944.25	1,500.00	3,015.00	2,400.00
6146 · Church Banquet	0.00	0.00	0.00	12000
6147 · Church Representation	0.00	3,700.00	3,035.00	2,735.00
6239 · Men's Fellowship (Laymen) Exp	0.00	0.00	0.00	
6275 · Outdoor Worship/Picnic	3,467.26	3,500.00	4,264.50	4,200.00
6276 · Vacation Bible School	1,102.74	1,200.00	475.57	489.84
6295 · Revival Expenses				
6296 · Fall Revival Expenses	2,700.00	4,000.00	2,600.00	2,881.00
6297 · Spring Revival	3,300.00	4,000.00	2,812.91	3,037.00
6295 · Revival Expenses	0.00	0.00	0.00	
Total 6295 · Revival Expenses	6,000.00	8,000.00	5,412.91	5,918.00
6325 · W.C. Sample Scholarship	1,500.00	2,400.00	2,988.08	2,400.00
6622 · Special Day Expense	24,633.48	25,000.00	2,113.20	2,177.00
6628 · Special Day Expense B			26,848.38	27,654.00
6834 · Men's Retreat	9,079.84	8,000.00	9,687.00	10,500.00
6043 · SPECIAL DAYS EXPENSES	1,852.17	0.00	150.00	0
Total 6043 · SPECIAL DAYS EXPENSES	49,579.74	53,300.00	57,989.64	70,473.84
6045 · BANK CHARGES EXPENSES				
6120 · Bank Service Charges	113.00	300.00	1,953.00	1,681.00
6048 Adjustments			200.00	
6121 · Returned Checks	6,860.50	500.00	2,871.50	1045
6122 · Safe Deposit Box	100.00	100.00	85.00	85.00
6045 · BANK CHARGES EXPENSES			807.65	0
Payroll Expense	3,244.41	3,500.00	0.00	0
Total 6045 · BANK CHARGES EXPENSES	10,317.91	4,400.00	5,917.15	2,811.00

6047 · BENEVOLENT	5,184.47	8,500.00	4,878.51	7,239.62
6050 · CHURCH MEMBERSHIP &TRAVEL EXPENSES				
6051 · CA State Baptist Congress of Ch	1,670.00	1,700.00	1250	7500
6083 · American Baptist Churches	1,500.00	1,500.00	700	1500
6084 · Bay Area Baptist District Assoc	1,500.00	2,000.00	1000	1,500.00
6085 · California State Baptist Assoc	6,726.37	5,000.00	7548.56	8000
6327 · Southern Marin Bible Institute	0.00	500.00	0.00	500
6086 · Nat'l Bapt. Convention	3,934.38	3,600.00	2424.8	3000
6087 · Nat'l Bapt Congress			800	1000
6088 · California Southern Baptist	0.00	250.00	0	0
Total 6050 · CHURCH MEMBERSHIP &TRAVEL EXPENSE	15,330.75	14,550.00	13,723.36	23,000.00
6053 · CHURCH PROPERTIES				
6200 · Interest Expense	72,174.29	72,175.00	65,591.91	72174.36
Loan Principle	119,215.07	19,215.00	79780.05	19215
Total 6200 · Interest Expense	191,389.36	91,390.00	145,371.96	91,389.36
6300 · Repairs				
6303 · Repairs A	830.65	1,000.00	20.97	2,000.00
6304 · Repairs B	2,105.00	1,000.00	275.00	6,000.00
6677 · Repairs C	9,773.27	1,000.00	0	1,000.00
Total 6300 · Repairs	13,208.92	4,000.00	295.97	9,000.00
6305 · Exterminator	916.00	1,000.00	840	950
6647 · Taxes - Property	7,715.69	8,000.00	11102.87	11,500.00
Total 6053 · CHURCH PROPERTIES	213,229.97	104,390.00	157,610.80	112,839.36
6055 · INSURANCE EXPENSES				
6180 · Worker's Compensation Insurance	13,186.76	13,000.00	13,314.14	13000
6185 · Liability Insurance	12,776.00	9,500.00	13,487.00	10215
6190 · Disability Insurance	895.56	950.00	895.56	2170
6058 Van Insurance Expense	1,175.75	950.00	934.50	935
Total 6055 · INSURANCE EXPENSES	28,034.07	24,400.00	28,631.20	26,320.00
6057 · LOVE GIFTS, DONATIONS, MISSION				
6057 · LOVE GIFTS, DONATIONS, MISSION				
6111 · Hurricane Relief			7,986.50	2000
6243 · Mission Support	4,658.00	5,500.00	10,225.00	5000
6455 · Visiting Ministers	1,300.00	600.00	2800	2,800.00
6475 · World Vision	416.00	500.00	659.00	800
6646 · Love Gift	13,412.87	3,700.00	8,502.00	5,000.00
POI Donation	5,000.00	0.00	0.00	0
Total 6057 · LOVE GIFTS, DONATIONS, MISSION	24,786.87	10,300.00	30,172.50	15,600.00
6060 · EXPENSES MISCELLANEOUS				
6240 · Miscellaneous Expense	164.40	150.00	1,380.25	1300
6071 · Leadership Workshop Expense	300.00	500.00	816.00	840.50
6072 · Staff Meeting Expense	484.57	600.00	1,054.59	1,086.23
6078 · Staff Retreat	597.79	700.00	600.47	700.00
6079 · Joint Board Retreat	1,501.41	2,000.00	2209.22	2,300.00
666. Wednesday Night Service				4,000.00

6128 · Ministry Fair Expense	0.00	1,500.00	271.52	300
6150 · Depreciation Expense		0.00		
6160 · Dues and Subscriptions	438.00	550.00	2349.68	2300
6175 · WC Sample to POI Scholarships	603.65	2,400.00	0	
60 Youth Training and Development				8000
6172 · Flowers	1,179.56	1,500.00	835.47	861.00
6251 · Baptismal Expense	357.02	400.00	0	200
6221 · Loan Fees	1,725.00	0.00	0	0
6230 · Licenses and Permits	156.00	200.00	208	250.00
6556 · Marketing	280.50	400.00	125.00	150.00
Total 6060 · EXPENSES MISCELLANEOUS	7,787.90	10,900.00	9,850.20	22,287.73
6063 · OFFICE EQUIPMENT				
6226 · Internet Service Provider	1,019.29	1,000.00	1,017.35	1,000.00
6233 · Copier	5,375.73	6,300.00	5,801.41	6,800.00
6235 · Postage Equipment	2,104.66	2,600.00	2,771.20	2,300.00
6236 · Postage Machine Postage	871.65	1,000.00	828.57	839.12
6244 · Satellite Expense	1,100.00	1,200.00	1,100.00	1,100.00
6260 · Printing and Reproduction	508.61	500.00	189.26	200.00
6675 · Personal Computer	3,879.98	1,000.00	0.00	1,000.00
6680 · New Furniture	161.29	1,000.00	0.00	500.00
6063 · OFFICE EQUIPMENT	0.00	1,500.00	164.59	200.00
Total 6063 · OFFICE EQUIPMENT	15,021.21	16,100.00	11,872.38	13,939.12
6067 · SALARIES/BENEFITS				
Total 6067 · SALARIES/BENEFITS	338,762.63	413,391.32	359,934.54	462,171.48
6070 · SUPPLIES EXPENSES				
6554 · Janitorial Supplies	746.39	1,000.00	1128.42	1162.27
6555 · Supplies			5754.18	5927
6070 · Supplies	1,450.43	5,000.00	0	
Total 6555 · Supplies	1,450.43	5,000.00	5,754.18	5,927.00
6557 · Office	4,833.64	5,000.00	6755.08	6772.15
6558 · Kitchen Expenses	0.00	0.00	0	
6070 · SUPPLIES EXPENSES	4,839.61		0	
Total 6070 · SUPPLIES EXPENSES	11,870.07	11,200.00	13,637.68	13,861.42
6075 · TRANSPORTATION EXPENSES				
6229 · Vehicle License/Registration	250.00	250.00	0	250
Total 6075 · TRANSPORTATION EXPENSES	250.00	250.00	0.00	250.00
6080 · EXPENSES OTHER			0	
6167 · Emergency Expenses		18,000.00	0	18000
Total 6080 · EXPENSES OTHER	0.00	18,000.00	0.00	18,000.00
6270 · Professional Fees				
6280 · Legal Fees	105.72	500.00	588.81	600.00
6270 · Professional Fees	0.00	0.00	0	0
6650 · Accounting	1,455.00	850.00	4,150.00	4275
Total 6270 · Professional Fees	1,560.72	1,350.00	4,738.81	4,875.00
6310 · Maintenance and New Equipment				
6228 · Maintenance & Operations Expense	5,555.60	5,500.00	4341.82	5000
6171 Equipment exp			2334.97	
6301 · Electrical Expense	0.00	1,000.00	2,812.63	2900
6234 · Alarm System	1,272.00	1,300.00	1,272.00	1,300.00

	6571 · Elevator			2,924.00	2,717.43
	6310 · Maintenance and New Equipment	3,819.42	4,000.00	4610.73	2829
Total 6310 · Maintenance and New Equipment		**10,647.02**	**11,800.00**	**18,296.15**	**14,746.43**
6350 · Travel & Ent					
	6351 · Conference Expense		500.00	0	0
	6370 · Meals	1,717.16	500.00	2316.47	2,385.00
	6380 · Travel Members	612.60	600.00	0	0
	6381 · Lodging Expense	5,461.96	4,000.00	5677.15	5,847.00
	6350 · Travel & Ent	447.65	2,500.00	8475.88	8,730.00
Total 6350 · Travel & Ent		**8,239.37**	**8,100.00**	**16,469.50**	**16,962.00**
6390 · Utilities					
	6400 · Gas and Electric	14,038.58	15,000.00	13894.23	16,172.78
	6401 · PG&E 227 N. Grant Street	536.46	0.00	0	0
	6403 · PG&E 910 Mt Diablo			551.8	700
	6410 · Water	1,653.66	1,600.00	2102.16	2,000.00
	6411 · Water 227 N. Grant St.	223.02	300.00	0	0
	6412 · Water 154 N Grant			352.9	350
	6413 · AT&T	347.42	350.00	0	0.00
	6414 · Paging Service	4.44	0.00	0	0.00
	6415 · SBC	8,882.50	5,500.00	214.24	0.00
	6417 · Telephone/Fax/Cable Service	500.94	550.00	6119.74	6,304.00
	6420 · Garbage	4,186.61	4,500.00	4020	4,200.00
	6421 · Cellular phone	1,726.20	1,000.00	850.33	1,000.00
Total 6390 · Utilities		**32,099.83**	**28,800.00**	**28,105.40**	**30,726.78**
6418 · Van Expenses		350.00	500.00	866.77	1,000.00
6470 · Workshop and Training		520.00	0.00	375	1,000.00
6658 · Members appreciation		0.00	1,100.00	0	1,500.00
6575 Gas Expense				65.88	100.00
Taxes- Other				10	
6887 Reimbursed POI				2319	
6999 · Uncategorized Expenses			0.00	0	0
7000 Reserve Funds			65,545.68	0	35170.91
				0	
Total Expense		**844,217.18**	**895,317.00**	**858,325.86**	**1,011,027.30**
Net Ordinary Income		-24,994.68	-19,215.00	44,260.44	0.00
Net Income		-24,126.08	-19,215.00	44,260.44	0.00

Working Session

Utilizing the S.W.O.S. Method, we were asked to break off into groups and discuss issues and explore ideas to resolve issues in our church.

S—Strengths

W—Weaknesses

O—Opportunities

S—Strategy

GROUP ONE
TEAM SPIRIT

STRENGTHS

1. Diversity—Different background and knowledge levels.
2. Flexibility—Everyone is active in other ministries of the Church.
3. Dedication—High commitment level and strong support of the Church.

WEAKNESSES

1. Ability to take risks and except change to become more effective.
2. Able to come to an agreement without being in agreement. If we are not unified, how can we expect the Church to be unified?
3. Fear to address difficult issues as they relate to individual feelings.
4. Developing people, no system is currently in place.

OPPORTUNITIES

1. We must seize the young people and get them involved to take us to the next level.
2. We must not take the Pastor for granted, we must take advantage of the great man we have.
3. The music department must get involved in the leadership, recruitment and commitment to elevate the level of our music ministry.

STRATEGIES

1. Fellowship outside the church. Outreach.
2. Lead by example.
3. Encourage the congregation to stay on the path of Christ.
4. Constant training of officers to provide leadership.
5. Refocus on our purpose to handle the business of the church, to make decisions which are in the best interest of the church.

GROUP TWO
CHURCH'S IMAGE IN THE COMMUNITY

STRENGTHS

1. Proactive Church.

2. Community oriented Church.

3. Sense of history and great name recognition.

4. Politically active and strong leadership.

5. Flexibility (Not purely traditional.)

6. Teaching and Prayer Groups.

WEAKNESSES

1. Flexibility

2. Lack of follow-up.

3. Commitment

4. Failure to communicate the churches ministries.

5. Too often we take "NO" for an answer.

6. Too many meetings and events that serve no purpose.

7. Active "Rumor Mill"

8. Members not participating in the vision.

9. Challenges go unfulfilled.

OPPORTUNITIES

1. Re-activating the Courage Ministry and Singles Ministry

2. Take part in activities.

STRATEGIES

1. Stay in touch with others.

2. Fellowship hour after church.

3. Be responsible, live an upright life.

4. Avoid cliques and discouraging comments by confronting negativity head on.

5. Witness and evangelize.

6. Study the word, so we are able to share it with others.

GROUP THREE
DREAM TEAM

STRENGTHS

    1. People with lots of ideas.

    2. We perform well when dealing with short-term goals.

WEAKNESSES

    1. We fail to use what we have.

    2. Poor risk takers.

    3. Show lack of faith when working together.

    4. We look at congregational needs before community needs.

    5. Members in the church operating with the wrong motives.

OPPORTUNITIES

    1. Create intentionality in ministry.

    2. Enhance creative thinking.

    3. Cultivate new ideas/new ministries.

STRATEGIES

    1. Buy into goals, commitment and accuracy.

    2. Monthly meeting. (All ministries together.)

    3. Bring all ministries in line with CDM

    4. Marketing the good part of the Church.

GROUP FOUR
STRENGTHENING FAMILY RELATIONS

STRENGTHS

1. Long term marriages.

2. Long term members.

3. Longevity of Church and credibility in community.

4. Financial ability to care for families

5. Assistance to Young People.

6. Caring people with skill to assist others.

7. Scholarships available for young people.

8. Strong Benevolent Committee.

9. Skilled people in key places.

10. Strong Spiritual Leadership.

WEAKNESSES

1. Not providing the assistance needed in Singles Ministry.

2. Lack of fellowship among members.

3. Fear of sharing our problems.

4. Issues of spousal and child abuse are not addressed.

5. Little or no parenting skills.

OPPORTUNITIES

1. Share with other ministries.

2. The church provides referrals to marriage and family therapist.

STRATEGIES

1. Church can provide training through marriage and family workshops.

2. Members must take advantage of opportunities presented.

<u>GROUP DISCUSSION</u>

1. How do we communicate effectively with the whole congregation?

2. How do we discover hidden talent in the congregation?

3. How do we get peripheral members involved?

4. How do we grow toward a fully tithing congregation?

5. How do we disciple every member?

6. How do we inform the Bay Area about our church?

7. How do we raise the excitement level in our church?

Theme: "Re-Tooling Our Ministry for Maximum Efficiency"
GROUP EVALUATION

A. Pastor

B) Deacon Ministry

C) Trustee Ministry

D) Secretary

E) Administrative Assistant

F) Clerk

Theme: "Re-Tooling Our Ministry for Maximum Efficiency"
GROUP EVALUATION

Strengths:

Weaknesses:

Opportunities:

Strategy:

SAMPLE MINISTRY LEADERS SELF-EVALUATION
By Dr. Larry Wayne Ellis

Auxiliary Name_____ Leader_____

Responsibilities:	January	February	March	April	May	June
• Regular Church Worship Attendance						
• Regular Tithes and Offering; Leadership Offering as Requested						
• Regular Pilgrim Bible Study or Other Bible Study with Believers						
• Regular Sunday School Attendance						
• Regular Church Prayer Meeting Attendance						
• Regular Attendance at Workshop Training and Development Sessions						
• Attendance at Quarterly Business Meetings						
• Regular Participation in Other Church Ministries						
Comments:						

A Holistic Approach to Church Leadership August 2001